DRIVE SAFE
BE SAFE

I0504204

S. SUBRAMANIAN

INDIA · SINGAPORE · MALAYSIA

Notion Press

Old No. 38, New No. 6
McNichols Road, Chetpet
Chennai - 600 031

First Published by Notion Press 2019
Copyright © S. Subramanian 2019
All Rights Reserved.

ISBN 978-1-68466-863-2

Disclaimer

This book is written with sole purpose of making the reader, a better and safer road user in any form. They will be ensuring their own safety as well as safety of other road users. Guide lines and suggestions given in this book are very valuable, and will definitely be useful in normal times as well as in moments of emergency.

HOWEVER The author does not assume any responsibility of success of the procedures and methods enumerated in this book, as human perception and psychology varies from person to person.

Readers are advised to verify the latest rules and regulations in force from concerned competent authorities and take appropriate action as required.

The contribution of Reader's digest in Road Safety is Significant. They are well Researched and worth reading and emulating. I have taken contents from real life incidents 'Stolen car, Medical Miracle, Sixteen day ordeal of John vihtelic' My car won't stop and few jokes and end fillers and Good driver Astrological signs.' The sole purpose is to create a positive attitude in the minds of the readers on road safety.

Similarly certain interesting facts about rolls royce, Physiological outlook of various countries and interesting statistics on Auto mobiles, roads from sources like Guinness Book of world records and other sources. They will give lots of insights about auto mobiles to readers.

And from an old calendar of United India Insurance Co., four illustrations are used. This will emphasise the need for road safety in the minds of readers. As pictures speak louder then words.

I am sure the readers will learn a lot from them.

This book is dedicated to my **Mother** who blesses me always, and my dearest wife **Jai,** my daughter **Sukanya** and son-in-law **Murali** who laid solid foundation for this book and my younger sweet daughter **Krishna** and Son-in-law **Susi** for their valuable help and my grand sons **Sujay and Vishan** for inspiring me to write this book.

Sheer weight of various sources, like Newspapers, Television channels seminars and many real life incidents, precludes me from thanking them individually.

Contents

Pledge

I .... Will be from now onwards, A safe driver and Road user.

I will also render all possible help to the needy in the event of any unfortunate accident.

Personal Particulars

Name   :

Address   :

Telephone/Cell No   :

Office address   :

Telephone No   :

Vehicle details   :

Driving license no and validity   :

Name of insurance co   :

Policy details and validity   :

Blood group/special medical info   :

In case of emergency please inform   :

Name of doctor/relation and contact no :

Any other special information   :

Special Note to the Readers

Right now you are reading a very valuable book, which can change your lifestyle.

Select any chapter and read.

You will be inspired and get valuable tips to become a better and safer road user.

Keep this book handy. Revise and rerevise often.

You will develop confidence in setting an example to others.

In this book you will come across certain points which are repeated many times in different chapters. It is not an inadvertent addition. But deliberately added to emphasize their significance.

By being a safe and sane road user, your contribution to society, nation and your own family will be immeasurable.

GOOD LUCK

Preface

INDIA is **emerging** as the destination of choice in automotive and auto ancillaries industries, in design and manufacture.

The government had launched an ambitious 'AUTOMOTIVE MISSION PLAN' '2006–2016.' By 2016 automotive industry is set to contribute up to 10% of our gross domestic product of $145 billion (Rs. 5.6 lakh crores).

The phenomenal growth of the industry is going to thrust an extremely difficult responsibility on all future road users. The transport related problems would increase multifold with development.

Let us consider some important elements of human life connected with automotive industry.

Most essential part of life is breathing. We have to move around for our day-to-day work.

The foremost questions that should come up are: Are we breathing the air we should?

Are we able to move around safely?

The Answer for both is an empathetic No. Unfortunately the problems are only man made and hence the solutions also must come from man only.

One of the significant contributors to the above problems is Automobiles, which are responsible for both pollution and road accidents.

The spectacular increase in the number of motor vehicles on the road has created a major social problem. The loss of lives and serious injuries through Road accidents. The appalling human misery and serious economic loss caused by Road Accidents demand the attention of the society and call for the application of the solution to the problem.

Accidents do not happen, they are caused! Every year in India over

- 12,40,000 people are killed

- One Million people are injured

- 55,000 crore rupees is lost

- The human misery cannot be equated in terms of money alone

Pollution related deaths and loss of revenue to the state by way of sickness and medical expenses, is another significant factor. As per the study carried out by competent agencies in Delhi, 2500 people died in road accidents in 2017, and in the same period 12300 people succumbed to pollution related diseases. The figures are really frightening.

This is the scenario of **today.** Facing future problems related to transportation is going to be a very tough task for all future road users. We may not be able to have all round development, which will significantly reduce the gravity of the problems.

All drivers in future will be spending more time on the road due to traffic congestion and urban sprawl. This will definitely add stress to their daily lives and will result in waste of time and resources and reduce commuter safety, and add to the emission problems. The total distance traveled by all drivers will increase considerably, and this will offset any gain achieved by fuel economy and other technological developments. Uncertain human behavior and explosive growth of automobiles will also pose serious challenges to the future road users.

There is another fall-out, serious economic loss due to congestion of traffic. It is estimated that in MARYLAND USA the loss due traffic congestion, will be more than 3 billion dollars (about 1000 crore rupees). Every year. We do not have the correct mechanism to work out such loss. But we also lose substantial amount. This is besides loss due to accidents and pollution related losses.

All such factors will significantly contribute to avoidable losses. A developing nation like ours cannot afford to ignore such a huge loss. In this aspect prudent, safe use of vehicles, and its maintenance and upkeep will play an all-important role.

The stress of daily commuting to work and spending long hours on roads and late night shifts will become the root cause of many psychological problems. In many cases this may result in divorces and separation of family members. This will be a heavy price future citizens may have to pay for enjoying the fruits of development.

There is an urgent need to address these issues. All possible solutions must be thoroughly analyzed. Whatever be the solution, it is the implementation that counts and matters. A workable link must be established amongst all road users, which will bring benefits to all.

The purpose of this book is to infuse the concept "Drive Safe – Be Safe," in the minds of all readers. Many books have been written about this, but you will find this book is special and unique in many aspects. This book is a guide and companion for all readers in understanding the complexity of the problem and to become part of the solution… In short THIS IS AN ACTION BOOK and any action however small will have an impact on the society now and in future. This is like planting a small seed of a banyan tree, which is smaller than a chilli seed now, which will grow into a huge banyan tree in future.

In this book a radically different approach is adopted. This is the first of it's kind for every type of road user and a constant guide for every occasion now and in future.

The main theme of the book is **"You are the only person, who can and who should ensure your own safety."**

The book is

- Not exhaustive but comprehensive.

- Informative without being over whelming.

- The focus is on what you should know and what you should do.

Certainly this is not for theoretical knowledge, but practical implementable recipes, which are bound to bring results.

You have this book with you right now and you are reading it. With this beginning, you are becoming a part of the solution immediately.

It requires hard and consistent efforts to reach and maintain the state of safety.

Together let us make a sincere effort, to become a safe and considerate Road user.

Let this be a small step towards the great leap of a nation, free from transport related problems.

Good Luck to all Readers.

* * * * *

What This Book Will Do for You

When you board an Aircraft they give you a set of safety instructions on safety in air travel. There is a remark "read this now in leisure and understand them instead of reading in a hurry is case of emergency later."

Likewise knowledge of all transport related issues is a must for all road users, as you do not know when you will be required to use them.

We are all road users, irrespective of our place of living, social status, sex, religion, age etc.

Are you safe, as you want to be? This is a million rupee question?

The rules of safety are so simple that no one is observing them. But it is more likely you are not using them, and chances are neither your friends. They take the rules to be too simple to be followed.

There is no truly unavoidable accident. All accidents are/were preventable. This book is written precisely keeping you (the road user) in mind. I have made a sincere attempt to compile all transport related issues in the form of a single useful digest.

This book

- Is a guide for every road user in normal times as well as in moments of crisis.

- Deals with technical, economical, Social, psychological, medical, legal and other aspects.

- Is full of real life incidents, facts and anecdotes. Brings home to the road user in any form, the necessity to ensure their safety.

- Is written in simple English, easy to read, understand and follow.

Accident is defined as a sudden and unexpected absence of purpose in a regular succession of events. Very true. Aftermath of an accident can never be predicted.

By the time you finish reading this book, please take it from me, you would have developed a new respect for you and commitment to be a better road user.

Fore-warned is forearmed. You may be a driver, co driver, passenger, pedestrian, police official, doctor or a simple bystander witnessing an accident, directly or indirectly involved in one.

Whatever be your role, this book is a companion and a guide for you.

Using this you can become a better driver, better road user in any form and a person of better understanding.

Remember we are talking about your safety and not others.' You are responsible for it. As said earlier, the responsibility is fundamentally yours. I hope this book will help you in exploring the often perplexing and ever changing world of automobiles and human behavior with regard to accidents.

Accidents can happen to any body. Every life lost in accidents is precious, and matters to some one dear and affect their lives.

The affected person's family is put to untold miseries and financial and emotional strain. All of them could have been avoided, with some fore thought and timely action. Remember accidents don't discriminate victims.

Similarly pollution: whether you are a lawmaker or lawbreaker, you cannot avoid ill effects of pollution. You may be thinking of some temporary gains by way of reduced expenses.

Remember, pollution kills more persons than accidents. Always remember, your own health will be affected by pollution. You will be indirectly creating a generation of unhealthy people and the ill effects will continue to haunt the future citizens of the nation… We are morally and ethically responsible to hand over a pollution free atmosphere to our future generation.

But action speaks louder than words. What is required and expected of you is action and not just a cognizance or knowledge.

This book is a guide, constant companion, an insurance tailor-made for you for your own health and safety.

You may be the road user in any form, be safe, and never take chance. You are the only one who can ensure these for yourself.

This book will turn you into a problem-solver. Reread the pledge given in the beginning of the book once again and **gear yourself into action.**

Driving

The main business of driving is driving and driving alone and nothing else. Every one's safety is in the hands of the driver. Careless driving can cause accidents at any speed. Drivers have an obligation to society to do all they can to prevent any form of accident.

This is the most important chapter of the book, and also the main theme of the book.

It will be appropriate to begin this with a real life story.

100 Years and Driving

Elmen Leven Decker does not drive as often as he once did, and rarely at night.

But at the age of 100, he still backs his red and white Cadillac out of the garage a few times a week to go to grocery stores as to meet friends over lunch at a game of bridge.

He is one of the 44 centenarian drivers of Missourians (USA) who still possess a valid driving License.

He began driving about 80 years ago over bumpy gravel cobble stone streets. His first car was a 1918 Buick Roadster and costed $ 100. His second car was 1924 Chevy Coupe. In 1990 he bought his latest vehicle Cadillac Seville. He got his driving License renewed in July 2000, after passing vision test. His date of birth is November 3, 1900.

22 July 2000.

The above is given as an example of how a driver can drive safe and be safe at any age. Can any other history be more exemplary?

Driving a Motor vehicle is a privilege and not a right. It takes skill, common sense, and thorough knowledge of the rules and regulations found in the law along with a **sense of anticipation and judgment.** Driving a vehicle is always a function of very active brain. Any form of distraction, will adversely affect the driver's ability to function and their reaction to different driving conditions. The main business of driving is driving and driving alone; nothing else.

Every one's safety is in the hands of the driver. Drivers have an obligation to society to do all that they can to prevent accidents. This means constant checking for possible troubles while driving. While you are on the road care of your vehicle is up to you. Careless driving can cause accidents at any speed. Take care of your vehicle, cargos, passengers, and pedestrians and motoring public.

A good driver may not be always a safe driver. It is very difficult to define an ideal driver. He/She should be safe, economical, considerate to all fellow road users. At all times he must possess these qualities without any let up or hindrance. Every moment of driving is important. It is calculated that accidents are formed in a fraction of a second; in most of the cases accidents had already occurred, before those who are involved realized it. It is a Golden Proverb' "Accidents do not happen, they are caused." There is no such accident, which cannot be prevented.

There is no false excuse for fatalities in India. The startling fact is while in USA there are 850 CARS for every

1000 persons, in India we have 11 for every 1000. Fatality rate in US is, 17 persons for 1000 vehicles, in India it is 61. Is it not mind-boggling?

This clearly shows the cause of the problem is not the vehicles alone, but all road users. Unless all road users are going to be self-disciplined and observe all traffic rules this problem cannot be tackled. We also have the dubious distinction of being second worst drivers in Asia second only to China.

A safe driver is an asset. He is at once a safe road user also. He/She can set an example by his/her excellent road-sense to all around. A safe driver should endeavor to remain a safe driver at all times. He/She should not succumb to any temptation to 'easy' but unsafe driving habits.

It is better to be patient while driving or using the road in any form, than be a patient in a hospital.

With increase in vehicle population every day, congestion on road increases, driver's responsibility is also increasing manifold. They can contribute a lot to road safety.

As per the study carried out extensively in various countries by professional Agencies, most accident-prone drivers are aged between 18 to 20 and 70 to 80. Safe drivers are between 50 to 60. Hence you can conclude that both teenagers and senior citizens suffer from age related problems.

Senior Citizens as Drivers

Every one of us is either a senior citizen or approaching that status. For all practical purposes all persons who are 60 years old and above are considered as senior citizens. Because of increased life expectancy the number of senior citizens are on the increase. Most pathetic fact is hardly 5% of them are financially independent and 95% have to work to earn their livelihood and hence must move on roads in some form. They deserve consideration in all respects. Because of their age they become at once, both the cause and consequence of accidents. Some of the problems of senior drivers are

Chronological Age alone does not accurately measure their functional abilities.

Their capabilities, knowledge and ability to function safely vary within the same age. They usually deny their abilities and skills are worsening with age.

They should avoid high-risk driving, night driving and driving in inclement weather like rain, storm, fog etc.

Fortunately in India, senior citizens as drivers are comparatively less because our social demands are much less than western countries. Now more senior citizens are using two wheelers as a means of transport, as two wheelers give them some independence in movements and they can avoid hardships of commuting in over crowded urban transport.

Some important factors affecting senior citizens as drivers: are

1. Older drivers are more cautious and sensible.

2. Unskilled, impaired, unqualified drivers come from all age groups.

3. Due to prejudice older people are often blamed for accidents.

4. With increased age, weakening of physical ability and slower reaction time.

5. Senior drivers involve in disproportionately high percentage of accidents.

6. Person's age should not be the criteria for determining whether they should be given driving license.

There are two important factors vision and hearing, which affect senior citizens.

Vision: Senior drivers (for all age group with less than 40% of normal vision) are more likely for accidents than normal vision drivers. Since vision forms parts of almost 90% of driving efforts, this is the most important factor.

They need more light to see in an overcast sky.

Increased difficulty, when changing focus from near and far Greater sensitivity to sunlight and glare.

Diminished peripheral vision. Color blindness.

They should get their eyes examined by qualified doctors regularly at least once in 3 months and wear prescription glasses regularly, and must wear good sunglasses.

Keep mirrors, wind shield glasses, headlights and other lights clean and in working condition at all times.

Hearing: Visit your doctor and have tests. Wear hearing aids when recommended.

Reduce or eliminate background noises while driving.

Use rear view mirrors regularly to Asses vehicle coming – from the side, behind. Avoid conversations, loud talk while driving.

Try to concentrate more while driving; as in every mile 20 major decisions are taken. Be alert.

Do not drive under stress. Do not talk or listen to Radio or CD intently as they, are distractions.

Never use cell phones while driving. Never drink and drive. Senior citizens will have more alcoholic effect with fewer drinks.

Never assume your right of way, follow all traffic rules. Check for latest traffic rules, diversions, rerouting.

Drowsy Driving

Sleep is like money you can spend more than you get and end up in debt. Persons of any age can end up with "Sleep debt."

To stop feeling hungry or thirsty, you need food and water. To stop feeling sleepy, our body can just turn off and go to sleep. That is what makes sleep so dangerous. It is outside of your control. Sleep debt, may be result of your not sleeping well for required time or due to sleep apnea, a disease which will make you a tired, irritable person even you are lying in bed for more than 8 hours in the night or any other form of sleep disorder.

Drowsy driving is surprisingly common. Particularly for senior citizens. By nature they sleep less. Most of them take medicines for various ailments. People who sleep for six or seven hours are nearly twice as likely to fatigue related accidents as those who sleep for eight hours and more.

Not sleeping for twenty-four hours prior to driving is akin to a legally drunk. Getting enough sleep and feeling absolutely fresh are the best ways to avoid drowsiness.

Causes of Drowsiness:-

1. Circadian rhythm. Body's urge to sleep is strongest from mid night to 6 A.M. and in mid afternoon.

2. Late night driving, long trip, lonely trips.

3. Alcohol even a small amount can increase fatigue and drowsiness.

4. Anti anxiety medicines narcotics can cause drowsiness.

5. Sleep apnea or other medical disorders. Never drive when you feel sleepy. Remember even one moment of distraction can cause an accident.

Effects of Alcoholic Drinks on Driving

Test among experienced drivers with two drinks with alcoholic concentration of 0.049% (much below the legal limit) has proved marked deterioration of driving performance by 25 to 30%.

Alcohol

A. Slows down reaction.

B. It creates false confidence.

C. It impairs concentration, dulls judgment.

D. It affects vision.

To avoid impairment in judgment

i. Never consume alcohol prior to and during driving

ii. Wait for half an hour after one drink

 iii. Wait for two hours after two drinks

 iv. Wait for four hours after three drinks

 v. Wait for six hours after four drinks

Remember Alcoholic effects reach the brain within five minutes after drinking.

Use your intelligence in pre spotting the hazards. Familiarize yourself with alcoholic effect on driving.

In case if you must drink arrange a non-drinking driver to take you home.

Do not stop on your way home for a quick drink.

Do not encourage any guests or friends to have a drink before going home. No to one for the Road please.

The effects of all bad drinking habits will have more damaging effects while senior citizens drive two wheelers.

Even though the ill effects of drinks, drowsiness over speeding and careless driving are mentioned in senior citizens role, it is equally applicable to all age groups in varying degrees of severity.

Indian government is seriously considering more stringent measures to contain drunken driving. As per recent decisions a drunken driver can be sentenced up to 10 years of imprisonment instead of 2 years as of now. Any fatal accident because of drunken driving will be treated as rash and negligent driving.

In addition the Government will be implementing following measures

 A. No speed breakers, or hoardings on highways so as to allow smooth traffic

B. All city transport vehicles will be fitted with speed governors

C. Each city transport buses will have to be insured so as to enable victim's kin to get compensation early

D. Fitting of cameras in strategic locations so that hit and run drivers cannot escape

Teen Age Driving

Teen age driving is as much an issue as senior citizen driving. Mainly because accident rate in teenage driving is much more and it is an international issue.

Majority of two wheelers are owned and driven by teenagers and persons below 30 years age.

Since minimum age required for getting a driving license is 18 years maximum persons try to get license on completion of 18 years of age.

In USA, all have to appear for a written test before getting learner license. So it is not uncommon to find maximum persons as soon as they complete 18 years throng license officer for writing the test. This test is simple in form and requires question and answers from a prescribed book, specially published by licensing authorities. Only whenYOU PASS THE TEST (sometimes after many attempts) you can apply for learner license. This gives them basic knowledge about various rules and regulations, driving methods etc.

After learning driving under supervision and passing the test by authorities, license is issued in three stages.

First: Drive vehicles during daytime only accompanied by a person having valid license.

Second: Drive vehicles during daytime only accompanied by limited number of passengers.

Third: Drive independently in day and night.

In spite of all these, accident rate in teenage driving is very high. Persons of age between 18–20 are more susceptible to accidents.

It is estimated every youth in USA is spending about $ 2490 dollars, (Rs. 1 lac) per year on drinks.

The condition of Indian teenagers may not be that bad, but similarity definitely exist.

What parents can do:

1. They should take interest in teaching teenagers about hazards of driving before they get their license.

2. First time drivers do not know how to act or react to other drivers on the road, pedestrians and distractions. Road banners are major distractions for teenagers.

3. Parents must provide a safe vehicle.

4. Review driving obstacles and situations in detail such as flat tires, brake, steering system failures in detail.

5. Show your teens newspaper clippings, share news about accidents and explain how it had occurred and how it could have been prevented. Particularly how accidents are caused by drunken drivers.

6. Take them to various Road safety campaigns and let them interact with others and understand significance of safe driving.

More safe driving tips:

Earlier drivers were taught to imagine their steering wheel was a clock and place their hands at 10 o'clock and 2 o'clock positions. HOWEVER STUDIES HAVE SHOWN THAT THE 8 O'CLOCK AND 4 O'CLOCK POSITIONS ARE SAFER AND ALLOW MORE CONTROL IN QUICK TURN SITUATIONS.

EXPERIENCE COUNTS. WHAT YOU MAY LACK IN REFLEXES, YOU MAY BE ABLE TO COMPENSATE FOR IN SOUND JUDGEMENT. MATURITY AND FORESIGHT CAN HELP YOU MINIMIZE RISK BY MAKING SIMPLE ADJUSTMENTS TO YOUR DRIVING HABITS.

High Way Driving

More than 70% of the traffic is on Highways. All drivers are likely to use national and state highways often may be as a part of the journey or full journey.

Remember most of the accidents occur in National Highways because of heavy and dense traffic. Again driver's negligence is the major cause. To be a good driver you need to see well. For that you must be alert to what is going on around you.

You must look down the road, to the sides and behind your vehicle and be alert for the unexpected events.

Do not take your eyes from the road more than few seconds at any one time.

Check often for speed limits and keep your vehicle within the range.

Going slower than minimum speed IS as dangerous as going at high speed. Most accidents occur involving two or more vehicles, when drivers go too fast or too slow than other vehicles on the road.

Over Taking

When you drive faster than other vehicles, you may have to overtake number of vehicles. Remember as per motor vehicles act, you are solely responsible for overtaking any vehicle. Take extreme care before, during and after overtaking so that you are not hindering movement of any other vehicle particularly vehicles coming from the opposite direction.

Stopping and Turning

Indicate your intention to turn or stop well in advance, so that vehicle coming behind and from opposite direction are well aware of it and act. Try to avoid panic stops as it forces the drivers behind you to stop without hitting your vehicle, which may not be possible at all times.

Watch out for highway hypnosis.

This is caused by same ness of road and traffic. The hum of the tires, engine, and wind also adds to the hypnosis. It can make you sleepy and unaware of the traffic around you. You can avoid this by constantly moving your eyes and watching. If you feel sleepy pull out of the highway and do not risk falling asleep at the wheel.

DO NOT OVERTAKE ON BRIDEGS, SCHOOL ZONES, PEDESTRIAN CROSSING & JUNCTIONS

Driving in Hilly Road

When you drive in Hilly and Ghat Road. You must sacrifice speed for safety. Always drive slowly and in proper gear and do not allow the engine to stall. Never try to over take particularly at bends. Watch for all cautionary signs every sign is vital and must be followed. Extreme care is required when driving up or down in hill roads for you will be using gears steering and brakes continuously.

Driving during Rains and on Snowy Surface

In both cases road surface will he wet and is known as aqua planeing, which will reduce the contact between tires and road.

For our own safety and for our family's sake we should consider safety as our watchword. Whether it rains or shines, whether we are driving in National Highways, Hill Roads or Rural Roads.

Whether you are driving at day or night remember:

1. Always drive defensively.

2. Never over speed or overload your vehicle.

3. Always be considerate to other road users.

4. Keep all papers of your vehicle up to date and valid.

5. Keep your vehicle in sound mechanical condition.

6. Never drink and drive.

7. Always safety be your prime consideration while driving.

8. Be in sound physical and mental condition before and during driving.

9. If riding two-wheeler never venture without helmets for you and your pillion rider.

10. Always try to help stranded vehicles and vehicles involved in accidents. Remember you also may need such help some time.

Different Aspects of the Driving Technique

A safe driver should drive well in normal conditions. He/she should also know how to drive under difficult conditions.

- Defensive driving to avoid making mistakes or being in an accident because of some one else's mistake.

- Keep your eyes moving. Notice what is happening around you.

- Expect – it almost as a rule with no exception – other drivers to make mistakes, or rather the probability of such a mistake is high. For example be ready to react if the other driver does not stop. Never cause an accident on purpose. Be considerate to human life.

- The way you sit and hold the steering wheel affects your driving posture. The correct posture is to sit with your back straight and relaxed against the seat.

- Move your seat close enough so that you can easily reach the pedals but far enough that your elbows are to your front when you hold the steering wheel.

- Keep both feet within reach of floorboard.

Indian driving conditions are entirely different in many aspects and demand special skills. We are also rated as one of the worst drivers in Asia.

Our major problem is the heterogeneous nature of our transport scenario like slow moving handcarts, animal drawn carts, and cycle rickshaws. All types of three wheelers headed by indisputable autos and sleek Mercedes E 220 S all plying on road at the same time. To drive vehicles under such handicaps can be felt only when one drives on the roads. Accidents that take place in cities are not noteworthy. The fact that there are so few is nothing short of a miracle. Probably the reason is that for traffic so bad that speeds are really low. Average speed of cars in Mumbai is said to be around 8 to 9 Km per hour because of roads getting clogged due to congestion.

It also explains why accident rate is very high in the national and state highways, because the drivers feeling suddenly relieved of congestion at the city outskirts and speed up beyond their capabilities at least just to give vent to their suppressed feelings, if not anything else.

While stopping the vehicle, anticipate for all traffic and road conditions. While braking, two main factors are involved. First is known as reaction time and distance. When you notice an obstruction and decide to apply brakes the vehicle continues to move at the same speed till you **actually** apply brakes. This distance **increases** with speed. Then when you actually apply brakes the vehicle slows down to a stop. Following is a comparison.

vehicle speed	Reaction Distance	Braking Distance	Total stopping Distance
45 Km	100 Feet	90 Feet	190 Feet
80 Km	176 Feet	284 Feet	460 Feet

Speed has increased by two times (approximately) but total stopping distance by more than, 2.5 times. So vehicle speed is an important factor.

In the present and future generation vehicles, lots of safety features on brake system, like anti lock brake system, fail safe brakes, ceramic ventilated disc brakes, non fading brake linings etc are getting added. They make brake systems more effective and fail proof.

In commercial vehicles air operated brake system is used. The system will operate only when the air pressure in the system is above certain predetermined level. If pressure drops below the predetermined limit due to leakage or any other reason, the system will become mechanically operated and will lock the drive wheels. So future drivers of trucks and buses cannot offer 'brake failure' as the reason for accidents, as the system is 'FAIL SAFE.' What the driver would have done is, "he would not have applied brakes at all and falsely claim that brake had failed."

But the driver continues to be the most important person, who can make the system effective. An experienced, alert, healthy driver will react to a potentially hazardous situation, and take required action.

The reaction time includes recognition of the hazard, thought and movement of the right foot onto the brake pedal. It will be in the order of 0.5 second for an alert, healthy and experienced driver. Any momentary lapse of the driver will increase the reaction time and will make all the difference between SAFE and UNSAFE braking.

Horns

Horns are provided in vehicles for forewarning others and drawing their attention. They should be used with care and wisdom. Do not use horn to establish your right of way.

It becomes an unwanted distraction and other road users are literally drawn into accidents. Similarly using horns with very high decibel sound not only causes sound pollution but also scares people into accidents.

Night Driving

Driving during nights is more difficult than during the daytime. The headlights of on coming vehicles pose serious problem of glaring right on eyes and your own headlights limit your view of side of the road.

For driving in night you should

1. Make sure windscreens and windows are clean.

2. Turn on your head light ½ hour after sunset and off ½ hour before sunrise.

3. Make sure your headlights are clean and working well and properly focused.

4. Use dipper whenever you see vehicle coming in front. It will help and be good for both.

5. Slow down when you approach a curve.

6. Use the edge line on berm as guide. This is absolutely important when you are driving on hill roads.

7. Stay awake and alert do not drive when you feel tired.

8. Watch for all Road signs. They are **important** for driving.

9. Watch carefully for stranded cars and people on either side of the roads.

Driving on Wet Pavement

When it starts to rain, water mixes with dust and oil on the road to form a slick greasy film. Fallen leaves can also become slippery. The brakes will not be effective because of poor grip. So reduce the vehicle speed to adjust to the condition, to avoid slipping at normal speeds.

Check the inflation pressure at least once in a week and correct it when necessary.

Have tires with deep treads, worn out and bald tires are most dangerous. 90% of tire-related accidents occur because of bald tires.

Recent serious hike in fuel prices is forcing many fleet operators to adopt unusual methods to reduce fuel consumption. One of them is to over inflate the tires, which is known as hyper milling. The tires are inflated almost double the recommended pressures. This is said to reduce the fuel consumption by about 20 to 25%. This may be a temporary gain but increases the risk of bursting of tires due to over heating and rapid tire wear and heavy damage to the roads because of over heated and over loaded vehicles. They become a potential danger to themselves and other road users.

The more you realize the importance and advantages of safe driving; you automatically become an exemplary driver. Our efforts must be to maintain that state and never succumb to temptations. Always remember there is no safe speed, alertness of the drivers will differ and reaction times will vary. You are the best judge to drive vehicle at a speed in which you will have total and absolute, control of the vehicle, anticipating the probability of everybody else's committing a mistake.

Special caution for drunken drivers: Thank your stars that you are not in san-Salvador. There, drunken drivers can be punished to death by a firing squad – (san Salvador is in central America).

How to Minimize Stress behind the Wheel

If you are one among the millions who commute to work every day in any type of motor vehicle, your respiration rate is likely to increase from 12 to 17 breaths per minute and your heart rate from 74 to 80 beats per minute.

An average commuter spends an equivalent of 1.5 weeks every year stuck in traffic; he drives from 12500 to 20000 Km every year (this may vary from country to country).

Traffic frustration leads to road rage, reckless driving. Stress is a personal phenomenon. No effort either short term or long term must be spared to control this aspect, which is normal to occur for any one. This problem will become more serious in future as driving distances will increase and time spent on roads will increase due to congestion of traffic roads and increased number of vehicles. This will lead to many psychological differences in families, which may increase divorces and brake up of families.

Rush hour – Rude drivers – Road construction. These three R's make stressful driving for every one especially for senior citizen drivers and road users.

Regular exercise, defensive driving and careful choice of vehicles (Cars, & Two wheelers) can help senior citizens compensate for their effects of aging.

Vision: Average 75 years old person needs about 3 times more light than a 25 year old to see the same object.

We cannot turn back the clock but we can get frequent eye exams, wear corrective lenses and plan responsibly.

In cars produced at present and in future cars many safety features will be fitted to help all drivers.

- Instrument panel with larger symbols and adjustable lighting.

- Automatic dimming rear view mirrors to reduce headlight glare.

- Rear window wipers.

- Wider, reflecting curbs and markers.

- Better city and highway lightings.

Effect of Medicines

Both prescription medicines and over the counter drugs can slow reflexes, Blur vision and cause drowsiness. Even cough syrups may have unexpected side effects. Drugs typically affect people differently at 60 when compared to the age 20, people tend to gain weight and loss of muscle tone, which changes the way chemicals are absorbed. Senior citizens will take longer to get rid of effects of drugs. Similarly combination of different medicines may cause harmful effect. Whether you drive any vehicle or use the road in any form, be careful about the side effects of the medicines you are taking as no body else will give any allowance for that nor give any compensation.

All road users particularly senior citizens whether they are driving a car, two wheeler or using road as pedestrians, must be aware of the effects of medicines they are taking.

Dosage, time (before or after meals). Those who are diabetic taking medicines on empty stomach and not taking food in time will have serious problems like dizziness, sunstroke easily. Even urgency to answer calls of nature, may affect actions considerably.

Always carry your short medical history, allergies, and details of side effects of medicines with you. They may be your lifesaver in case of emergencies.

Hanging identity cards around their necks for diabetics patients, especially who might run the risks of 'very low sugar'or 'very high sugar.' Will, be of great help in case of emergencies and patient may be unconscious.

Reversing the Vehicle

Remember, when you are driving, it might be nessarary to reverse the vehicle for parking or change direction. This is the part of driving test All reversing crashes are **preventable.** It requires just patience and common sense.

Take care while reversing and follow the procedure given below

1. Put your foot on brake and hold it till your vehicle is completely stopped and you have engaged the reverse gear.

2. Look back the entire time. Before reversing make sure the area is clear and nobody is in your way of reversing and no obstruction to your vehicle.

3. Reverse very slowly. The vehicle is designed to slow speed only during reversing.

Never reverse your vehicle

1. When you are in an crossing, or intersection of roads

2. When you have made a wrong turn

3. Across the traffic lanes

4. Into an intersection of roads

5. Around a corner of roads

6. When more numbers of vehicles are behind you

Parking of Vehicles

1. Decide in advance, about your stopping and parking

2. Give your intention about slowing down and parking to all other road users, in clear unmistakable manner

3. Never encroach other's parking rights

4. Make sure it is an authorized parking place

High-Risk Parking

1. Corners of inter sections

2. In drive ways of other road users

3. End spaces of shopping complexes

4. Near any turnings

5. Next to any vans

6. Un lighted road corners

7. Parking on hills without turning the, wheels of your vehicle, wheels should be turned towards the curb or shoulders when facing down the hill

8. Should be turned away from the curb when facing up the hill

9. Should be turned towards shoulder when no curb is available

Illegal Parking

1. Any cross walk, drive way or bridge.

2. Double parking

3. At bus stops

4. 20 feet from any intersection

5. 30 feet from any stop sign

6. On the wrong side of the street facing traffic

7. On notified No parking areas

Rear View Mirror

Using rear and side view mirrors:

Normally all vehicles are provided with one rear view mirror in the center and two side minors one on driver's side and other on non driver's side. You can call that as third mirror. In buses it is absolutely **essential,** so that the driver can watch passenger boarding and getting down.

Using the third mirror will improve your safety level to a very great extent. You can watch for errant drivers trying to overtake on wrong side.

Cameras mounted in inside rear windshield indicate positions of vehicles, which are coming from behind in a TV screen mounted on the dashboard. This helps driver in keeping safe distance. This is a feature in addition to rear view Mirror to help safe driving.

MIRROR INDUSTRY HAS PROVIDED A DRAMATIC DIMENSION TO SAFETY IN AUTOMOBILE INDUSTRY.

These mirrors reflect an extremely wide angle, there by covering a larger area with unparalleled clarity. They are distortion free; anti glare mirrors give the truest of reflections particularly at night, without straining human eyes.

Types various models to suit all two wheelers, four wheelers and heavy vehicles like trucks, buses are available.

Advantages

1. Reduction in Road accidents

2. Enhanced field of vision on the road

3. Improvement in view while changing lanes or while backing up

4. Anti glare properties

5. Increased pedestrian safety

6. Watching children in the Rear seat

7. Ease of installation

8. Maintenance free

9. Break resistant

Maintaining Your Vehicle

Good maintenance promotes safety. Driving habits determine maintenance needs.

Follow manufacturers' instruction for oil changing, and other maintenance intervals.

Check all fasteners for looseness or uneven positions, and disconnection.

Proper maintenance can keep your vehicle running, leaving you free to concentrate on driving.

There is no element of doubt about that no driver of a vehicle would like his/her vehicle should involve in any accident. Then accidents take place because the driver is the only factor that keeps on changing during the course of travel and any change in the driving pattern at any given moment also may be the cause of accident. Driving itself is a continuous process, where no reconstruction to possible.

The driver is the only person, who can, by his/her instant reaction to an impending danger can avert an accident.

A driver with couple of drinks can convert a docile luxury into a mad bull elephant.

There are three important conditions, which are interrelated road, brakes; and steering. Drivers can exercise control of brakes and steering systems according to road conditions.

Common points for both systems are the driver and the tires.

If both factors are in full coordination at all times and the systems are well maintained, it gives extremely safe conditions for driving at all times.

Worn out tires (bald tires) will nullify even well maintained system effect. Increase susceptibility to accidents. **Over speeding puts viciously unjustified responsibility on brakes, steering and human reflexes.**

In most of the cases the real cause of accidents, are not revealed due to the fear of rejection of claims, by insurance companies and penal actions by police and judiciary.

Statistics are at best amusing figures. They are a large collection of facts on any subject, their value has so changed that they are at best records of the past but useless, and even dangerous as a guide to the future. So blindly using statistics can be misleading. Statistics will not come to your rescue incase of accidents. One of the greatest leaders of our country said once that," Statistics is nothing but a careless and wayward collection of data followed by an attempt to carefully compute them."

Accident Related Facts

Proximate cause means the active efficient cause that sets in motion a train of events, which brings about a result without the intervention of any force started and working actively from a new and independent source.

Examples:

A. Due to braking of steering wheel, the vehicle collides with an external object and is damaged. Proximate cause is breakage of steering wheel.

B. The propeller fan of the vehicle flies off and damages the radiator, proximate cause is flying of propeller fan.

C. The body of vehicle gives way and shifting goods unbalance the vehicle resulting in over turning and damage. Proximate cause is giving away of body.

D. Loosening of the sun shade which falls on the bonnet and damage it. The proximate cause is loosening of the sunshade.

By regular maintenance and checks most of the proximate causes can be identified and rectified before the failures.

The Effect of Stress

The invisible effects of traffic jam on a driver in hurry.

A 34 year old man sitting for 16 minutes in a 1, 3 miles (3 Km) main road block.

His Blood pressure will increase by   30%

His pulse rate increase   30%   50%

Traffic Jam exercises to avoid stress

1. Clasp the hands. Then try to separate them without breaking the grip.

2. Press the knees together with hands still pressing try to separate the knees.

3. Draw a deep breathe, hold it and pull your stomach in for 10 seconds then relax.

Uneven brake attracts

Lights

Lights are the only means of communication between drivers in night. They all should be in working condition properly focused, illuminated as to indicate your position, intentions unmistakably, clear to all Road users, it enables you to see other vehicles, pedestrians, traffic signs, warnings clearly from safe distance.

Without proper lightings you are a potential risk for yourself, other road users, pedestrians.

Primarily for our own safety, we should keep all the lights in good working condition. Every light has a role while driving proper focusing of headlights is a must for safe night driving. Experience alone is not enough.

More about Brakes

A car has three braking systems. The accelerator, gear and the brake themselves.

A controlled well anticipated and unhurried act of slowing down or stopping will involve the use of all the three systems. The vehicle could be stopped very gently with least strain to both vehicle and driver. We can clearly observe this in trains; the driver anticipates stops, slows down and gently brings the train to halt at the exact position in the platform. This is a typical anticipated stop. We can learn from little kids, they get up and walk without any hurry and slow down and sit or some times fall very leisurely. They never hurt themselves. Your braking sequence should be exactly similar to children's walking.

Driving a vehicle safely and observing road etiquettes voluntarily are the best gifts we can give for both the present and future generations. All the future technological developments can be effective only when future drivers and road user follow the rules of safety. In this a good, safe-driving habit is a culture to be inhibited right from the basic training in a driving school.

As drivers and regular users of vehicles we can derive many benefits by

a. Joining automobile associations of various parts of INDIA like AASI, AAI etc.

b. Also become members of My TVS or similar organizations, which provide brake down services, and other medical, legal services.

c. This is in addition to having adequate and valid insurance coverage. The money we will be spending on these coverage will be a pittance when compared to the benefits, we can derive in case of any unfortunate accidents or major brake down.

Seat Belts and Childern's Seats

The culture of seat belts and children seats are slowly coming into force in all-INDIAN automobiles.

Children traveling in vehicles are exposed to danger of collision related accidents. In USA the children's seat is given more importance. In hospitals where the children are born, the authorities insist on children's seat in the car, as a pre-requisite before allowing the parents to take the child home… Similarly children are not allowed to travel in the front seats of the car.

Separate children's seat must be provided for them the parents are given special training to fix and remove the seats and also to maintain them.

Some of the instructions given regarding children's seats are given below.

1. Children 12 years and under can be killed by airbags in the event of collision, never allow them to travel in front seats

2. The back seat is the safest place for children

3. Never place a rear facing seat in the front

4. Sit as far as possible from the air bag

5. Always use seat belts and child restraints

Now we find seat belts have been compulsory in all vehicles and air bags are provided for driver's seat as well as passenger's seats. Child restraint seats will be introduced as standard fittings soon. We have a long way to go in implementation of the laws. Future cars and vehicles will have safety as most important consideration., and all safety related fittings will be standardized in all future vehicles.

All future drivers and commuters will be spending more time on the road due to traffic congestion and vast development of cities which will force people to travel more from their residence to their work place and markets etc.

The average distance traveled by each driver will increase considerably. Now average driver is driving 9000 kilometers every year. This will increase to 13000 to 14000 kilometers a year in next the 5 to 6 years. This will offset all gains by increased fuel economy and other technological developments. We may be back to square 1 or even may move to negative side.

Managing traffic in urban areas and highways is going to pose very serious problems to the authorities. But all drivers can contribute a lot by being themselves first a group of safe and sane thinking drivers. We can certainly reduce the burden of the state by our planning our journeys in advance and following golden principles of safe driving.

Most important aspect all road users must consider is cost of congestion in roads in peak hours or otherwise. We do not have a proper mechanism to work out the cost. Remember that this loss is in addition to the loss due to accidents. In MARYLAND USA it is estimated that cost of congestion had increased by 1200% since 1982, it is estimated that more than 3 billion dollars (approximately 1000 crores) is lost due to congestion every year. This is a recurring avoidable loss. Proper driving and prudent use of vehicles will go a long way in reducing if not eliminating the loss.

Motor Sports Racing

It will be of interest to know some details about the racing drivers and racing vehicles. They are a class apart in all aspects.

Most of the parts are designed individually to suit the racing drivers. The cockpit [driver's scat] is built around the mould of drivers' spine, rib cage and shoulders. The steering wheel, pedals, gloves, boots and overalls are custom made for each driver. The average cost of a racing car will be around 10 to 12 crore rupees.

The racing drivers undergo very tough and consistent training, which includes swimming, cycling, and rigorous exercises in gyms. They have to develop sufficient endurance level for racing.

They have to make sure they feel what the car is doing. This is much more than man machine relationship. Their job isn't just about driving, they should make sure the car is rightly set up, mechanically as well as technically and all computer controls are functioning properly.

When they drive the racecar, it becomes part of their central nervous system and, they in turn become an integral component of the car. The cars have over 100 sensors embedded in the chassis to measure engine performance, aerodynamics, oil pressure, brake lining wear and driver's performance etc.

The collected data is used in change of design or modifications, and plan for winning strategies. They also must form part of the entire team working for the racing sport.

Even though they are paid well (FERRARI pays around 47 million dollars to KIMI RAIKKONEN Rs. 175 Crores), they live very high-risk life.

We should learn some lessons from them, and develop more intimate relationship with our vehicles, which will make us better road users.

Before concluding this chapter, few points about employing drivers to drive your vehicle either part time or full time.

A. Whether you or any body else driving any vehicle, make sure that the person driving the vehicle is in possession of a valid driving license for the type of vehicle he/she drives. For example you may be having avalid driving license for a two-wheeler, but you cannot drive a car with that license.

B. This is as per the recent judgment given by the Supreme Court. It is the responsibility of the owner to ensure that the driver appointed by the owner or his representative to ensure that the driver is in possession of a valid license for the type of vehicle he is authorized to drive.

In case of failure to comply with this provision, the insurance company is not liable to pay any compensation. For any claim arising out of any accident the owner alone will be responsible to pay the awarded compensations to the aggrieved party.

According to the latest study about various causes of road accidents, the following interesting facts have been identified.

Women are better road users than men.

In 2005 men had 850 fatal accidents and 5697 serious injuries in road accidents, compared to 205 fatal and 1271 injuries suffered by women.

In 2006 men suffered 1166 fatal and 5467-injuries, compared to 170 fatal and 1255 injuries by women.

The above illustration should be an eye opener for all we should not feel shy to follow women as road users in all forms.

Another sad news is those younger generations between 25 to 40 years of age are involved in fatal and serious injuries in road related accidents, particularly when they are using two wheelers.

The following reasons are identified as main causes of accidents

1. Over speeding

2. Rash driving

3. Signal violation

4. Lane jumping

5. Driving without licence

6. Drunken driving

7. Violating U turns

8. Using cell phones while driving

9. Riding without helmets

Every detail we are getting, should teach us a lesson, which we should pass it on to our children and friends and all others whom we come into contact.

By being safe and a sane driver, we can set an example to our children, neighbours, friends and all others whom we will come into contact in our lives. Pollution free and accident free environment will be the best gift we can give to the future generation.

From now on let us become safe and sane road users in all respects.

* * * * *

The famous one-eyed general of ISRAIL Gen MOSHI DAYAN was driving at brake neck speed.

He was stopped by the Military Police and warned about his over speeding.

He replied 'I have only one eye my dear son, shall I concentrate on the Road or at speedometer.'

* * * * *

Are You a Good Driver

To find out how good a driver you are, take the following tests.

Test 1: Match the following conditions with your reaction.

Be Honest

A. Motorist ahead of you darting in and out in traffic.

B. You are behind an extremely slow vehicle and you cannot pass.

C. Another driver shouts at you and makes obscene gestures.

D. You are struck still in endless traffic jam.

E. A car you are trying to pass speeds up to block you off.

Your reaction against each situation from A to E.

1. Not at all angry. You are a saint

2. Barely ruffled, why get worked up

3. Fairly peeved. Your patience has limits

4. Check your radiator. You are ready to boil

5. Red flag on, you are ready to take on anybody in your way

    Max Scorable   :   25 (worst)

    Minimum Scorable :   5 (Best)

If your score is:

15 or less: You are cool in the cockpit' (best)

16–18: No angrier than an average Commuter

19–20: Breathe deeply. Calm down

20 or higher: You are a danger to yourself and others

Example: For condition A if your answer is 1 you score 1 mark. If your answer is 5 you score 5 marks.

Test 2 : Are you likely to have a car crash?

Some personality types are more prone to accidents than others. Consider the following statements to know you are in which category.

1. I seek a lot of advice over decisions

    a) Agree   b) Disagree

2. I like going to lively parties

    a) Agree   b) Disagree

3. It is usually best if changes occur gradually

    a) Agree   b) Disagree

4. I prefer to work on several problems at a time

    a) Agree   b) Disagree

5. I hate the loss of control produced even by moderate amount of Alcohol

    a) Agree   b) Disagree

6. When I finish something the details may still need check

    a) Agree   b) Disagree

7. I prefer to do things the way I was taught

    a) Agree   b) Disagree

8. More problems are caused by rules than by braking them

    a) Agree   b) Disagree

9. I am able to resist temptation when there is work to be done

    a) Agree   b) Disagree

10. I dwell more on likely gains than losses

    a) Agree   b) Disagree

Analysis

8 or more A's You score high as a safe driver and low in risk taking dare devils may scare you, but your insurance premium is being used for paying for this cranks.

5–7 A's you score below average for taking risks. You do not believe you have the special skills in risk taking.

3–4 A's you score above average for dangerous driving. You do not have enough contact fear of a crash to keep you safe.

0–2 A's you are to pursue excitement and kind of driver likely to have crash. You may be the center of attraction in dinner parties but you will miss few because you pushed the limits too for.

Bad Driver Signs

Whether you believe in astrology, or other wise, it will be of some interest for you to know the results of extensive study carried out linking astrological birth signs with driving habits.

From top down you go from worst to best drivers.

Sign

Libra	(Sep 23 to Oct 22) indecisive: craves consensus, flirtous. Lacks ability to make snap judgments necessary to avoid crashes.
Aquarius	(Jan 23 to Feb. 22) stubborn; rebellious, unconventional. Ignores the rules of the roads particularly speed limits.
Aries	(March 23 to April 22) risk taker, impulsive child like. Wants to race you off the line when lights turn green, demand right of way.
Pisces	(Feb. 23 to March 22) Day dreamers, theoretic, vulnerable. Does not pay attention, prone to road rage, and fishtailing.
Scorpio	(Oct 23 to Nov 22) vengeful, possessive, strong willed. Might chase you if you cut in front of them in their lane.
Taurus	(April 23 to May 22) Cautious, deliberate, stubborn. Has an urge to charge at red lights, fails to yield.
Sagittarius	(Nov 23 to Dec 22) Talkative, independent traveler. Argues with police, extreme driving, talking on cell phone at the wheels.

Capricorn (Dec 23 to Jan 22) Goal oriented, designing, traditional. So focused on the tradition they ignore speed limits and road signs along the way.

Virgo (Aug 23 to Sep 22) Analytical, skeptical, timid. Focusing on minor details (the squirrel) instead of big picture (speed trap).

Cancer (June 23 to July 22) Moody, nurturing, family oriented. Considers other drivers as extended family maneuvers car quickly.

Gemini (may23 to June 22) Alert, adoptable, curious. Need for mental stimulation helps them spot changing traffic patterns.

Leo (July 23 to Aug 22) Generous, egotistical, optimistic. Strives to be a star driver and be respected for it. Whatever be our star sign, we should just try to drive more like the ones from cancer down to Leo.

Truck and Bus Drivers

For our own safety and health, we should give them their due, which is legitimately theirs too.

We all have experienced the effect of rash and negligent driving of truck and bus drivers. Day in and day out we read in newspapers about numerous accidents caused by them.

But these categories of drivers are normally most misunderstood about their role. There are more than 4 million vehicles doing 3 million kilometers, every day.

More than 70% of the goods and passengers are being transported on roads.

Past impressions about them are

➤ They are rage bulls in china shop

➤ Dim witted adventurers

➤ Drunken brawls – speedster

Past problems:

➤ Used to spend most of the working hours, putting up with rugged road.

➤ Staying away from home.

➤ Doubling up as supervisors and labor.

➤ Rustling up loads for return journeys.

➤ Compromising personal safety by overloading.

➤ Always of risk of being waylaid and hijacked.

By staying away from home for long and to overcome boredom and monotony, they indulge in sexual malpractices. They have been identified as one of the main causes for spreading AIDS.

But modem trucks and buses are generations apart. The new generation driver's requirements are:

– Driving skills

– Technical Savvy (interest)

– Communication Skills

– Business sense

A good driver with five years experience can earn from 20000–25000 Rs. per month and can plan to own a vehicle in about 10 years time.

The new Volvo trucks are having state-of-art driver friendly system like

➤ Sleep warning

➤ Lane departure-warning

➤ Emergency braking

➤ Adoptive control

➤ Radar

➤ Camera based visibility to overcome blind spots

NEW GENERATION TRUCK

The picture of a new generation truck is given. Various sensors are placed in different parts of the truck, which generates data based on road, load, traffic density, weather etc. that are fed to a central electronic module. It processes the data and warns the driver in case of any emergency or automatically corrects required systems and regulates the vehicle function.

Bus drivers in cities have different types of problems. They have to be constantly alert. They have to take more than 20–30 major decisions during every one-mile of driving... Considering all such aspects; it is really a miracle that accidents are few.

Drivers are becoming more important in Trucks and buses with high performance potential. They are being given special training.

Volvo

They have 2.2 Km long driving track. The trainees are drivers with three to five years experience in heavy vehicles. They are taught theory, practical classes on safe driving, dynamic loading and unloading. Pass rates is 80%, so far more than 9000 drivers have undergone training.

Ashoke Leyland

10 Year old driving school in 2.5 acre training center complete with electronic signals, sign boards, road marking, and street lights for night driving. All conceivable configurations are provided. More than 1.2 Lakhs drivers have been trained so far. Trainee–Student Ratio 1:8.

Similarly other truck manufactures also train drivers.

The training has remarkable effect on overall performance and significant reduction in accidents. To quote one transporter with more than 100 tankers had 15 accidents per 100 vehicles in a year. After training the number of accidents has come down to one per 100 vehicles/year.

Government, manufacturers and other NGO'S are working out integrated trucking solutions to improve their efficiency.

The future drivers will be an integral part of the decision making process in all aspects of driving.

We are bound to see more educated people choose this profession (truck and bus driving).

Truck and bus drivers are road users like every one of us. We should learn to respect them as human beings, having emotions like every one of us.

With all round improvements in design, safety, knowledge, future truck and bus drivers will be more matured and well mannered... This may considerably reduce probability of accidents. But we have to make allowance for unpredictable human behavior.

For our own safety and health we should give them their due, which is legitimately theirs too.

* * * * *

In DELHI bus route 711 is very famous. It runs from janakpuri c-1 to lajpat nagar. One of the most crowded bus.

Once a passenger tried to climb the moving bus. The conductor scolded him saying 'why you are climbing the moving bus. You could get killed."

The passenger replied 'If I die, I will take rebirth and come back. If 711 goes I don't know whether it will ever come back.'

How the Automobile Works

Basically automobiles run on principles that are easy to understand as common sense. Automobile will not hurt you unless you go out of your way to hurt yourself. It is an engineering marvel.

Let us start this chapter with a small anecdote.

'One driver was taking a passenger on a highway. Suddenly the car started to run at brake-neck speed.

The passenger was scared and told the driver to control the vehicle.

The driver asked the passenger 'Do you know how to drive this vehicle?'

Passenger replied "No!

Driver did not slow down but repeatedly asked the passenger 'Do you know how to drive the vehicle?'

The passenger got very angry and shouted at the driver. 'When I ask you to slow down, you are not doing it and you are asking me whether I know how to drive the vehicle and I told you I do not know. Now stop the vehicle. I want to get down.'

To which the driver told, "I also do not know how to stop the vehicle. That is why I was asking you"

You can well imagine the outcome.

Many of us do not know the first thing about the machine we are licensed to drive.

Basically automobiles run on principles that are easy to understand as common sense.

Most of the devices on the vehicles will not hurt you unless you go out of your way to hurt yourself.

It is an engineering Marvel. The more you understand it, the more you will like it. An avenge automobile is like any other machine consisting of number of individual parts assembled together. It consists of about 8,500 parts including 1400 fasteners like bolts, nuts, rivets, cotter pins etc. All have been assembled in separate units and the units are compounded into a working form as we ultimately see.

The basic structure of the automobile more or less remains the same since original concept. There had been significant development in all aspects. Steel is one of the basic materials used, 160 separate distinct varieties of steel in more than 1000 combinations are used.

In addition, various materials like aluminum, copper, zinc, lead, rubber, plastic, cotton, wool, jute, nylon, leather, petroleum products, resin, turpentine, lead – to mention just the important ones and such other things are used for making an automobile.

The development in the material technology is continuous and ever changing.

Present as well as future cars must satisfy

- Market needs (customer's)

- Performance

- Economy

- Safety

- Comfort

- Convenience

- Reliability Social needs like

- Safety

- Environmental Protection

Constant research and developments are going on keeping the end user and society in mind.

The purpose of this chapter is to give the insight of working of various systems, keeping engineering details to the minimum requirement.

It will also provide some dos and don'ts to make the automobile a trusted and reliable companion at all times.

In the field of manufacturing automobiles and ancillaries India had attained world-class status in term of quality and quantity. Our vehicles and spares meet international standards and accepted all over. Government also encourages the industry as it helps in improving the economy of the nation.

Exports of automobiles and spares help in earning considerable foreign exchange.

Now, let us know some details of working of the automobiles, which will help us in understanding them as a trusted friend and companion.

Every automobile must have the following systems. The system is arranged in the order of importance from an owner's point of view

1. Electrical system, air conditioning

2. Power unit

3. Transmission system

4. Drive wheels

5. Steering System

6. Suspension System

7. Braking System

8. Coach work or body

9. Safety system

All Vehicles are manufactured conforming to the legal and customer requirements fully. But the responsibility to maintain it falls on the end user. All good and bad things happen because of good or poor maintenance only. Maintenance attention is an indispensable responsibility of the end user.

There is no free lunch.

For right action and wrong action.

We have to pay the price.

Yes, for no action also we have to pay the price.

So it is important for us to understand, the necessity for taking proper and correct action, and also understand the implications of wrong or no action.

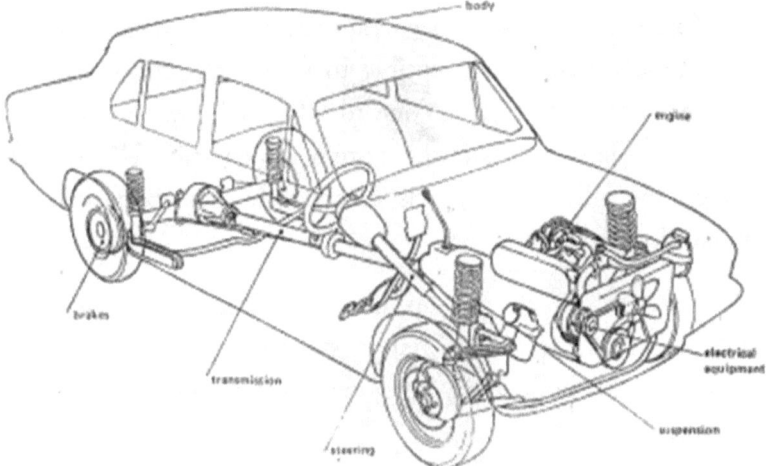

1. Electrical and Air Conditioning Systems:

From the owner's point of view this is the single most important system. The present and future generation vehicles are having/will have fully electrical and electronic control systems. More than 60%–70% of the vehicle controls are electrical and electronic. Most important point is in the case of electrical brake down, owner/driver may not be able to do anything. But by taking right action in following simple maintenance-care and checks he/she can prevent breakdowns to a great extent.

Most of the electronic systems are working on semiconductors, transistors, which are susceptible to minor changes in electric voltages. They also can fail due to what is known as **residual electricity.** This means if the system is not switched off even though the ignition switch is turned off, these parts can get damaged.

First: Ensure all systems like a/c, electrical gadgets and switches are switched off before/switching off the ignition. This must be done even when you are using keyless entry remote.

In the electrical system the most important component is the battery. In short battery can be called as the heart of the vehicle. More than 17% of vehicle breakdown occurs because of faulty battery. For effective functioning of all systems a fully charged battery is the primary requirement. A fully charged battery will have 12.6 to 13.2 volts.

The automotive battery is called 12 volts storage battery and reversible battery. It means the battery stores electrical energy and delivers when it is required and can be recharged to its original state.

Principles of Working

The battery is known as lead-acid battery, because lead and diluted sulphuric acid are used to produce electricity. The electrical energy is initially stored as electro-chemical energy. This type has lead plates, which are immersed in an electrolyte of sulphuric acid and distilled water (40% acid and 60% by distilled water).

Cell Action

As the battery discharges (gives up its energy) the lead in the plates undergoes a chemical change and the acid becomes weaker. (This is called discharging)

To reverse this action, an electrical charge is supplied from the alternator. This charges the lead plates back to the original chemical forms and strengthens the electrolyte. The charge current must pass through the battery in one direction only, so direct current (DC) is supplied with (+) positive terminal of the charger connected to the positive terminal of the battery. The negative or ground terminal completes the circuit.

The more we know about battery the more we will be able to appreciate its role.

The following explanation will clarify the maintenance aspects

B – **B**ody or container. Keep the container safe and secure

A – **A**cid – Never add acid. Top up with distilled water only

T – **T**erminals – keep them clean and free from corrosion

T – **T**ightness of clamps, wiring, terminals. Keep them clean, tight and dry

E – **E**lectrolyte level – check for correct level

R – **R**echarging keep battery fully charged always

Y – **T**hese things are to be done by **YOU**

By timely and proper maintenance most of the problems can be overcome.

When you switch on the ignition a myriad things happen at the same time

A. The battery starts supplying electricity to electronic control module, dashboard lights, gauges and electric fuel pump, which is actuated. The minimum voltage required is 12.1. If this voltage is not available, electronic control module will not function and **no system will work.**

B. The starter circuit on battery is prepared to deliver current up to 100 amps required for starting.

C. The battery also supplies current when the engine is not running and in case of emergencies and breakdown. For example hazard warning lights.

Most of the batteries are maintenance free and require very little attention. There are number of battery stations who will attend to battery needs free of cost or at a very nominal cost.

Removal of Battery

When you want to do any work in the vehicle it will be safer to disconnect the battery to prevent accidental starting of the vehicle by some body else. Always disconnect the negative terminal first.

This (ground) will prevent short-circuiting and prevent fire hazards in petrol engines due to sparking.

How to identify positive and negative terminals.

1. Normally positive terminals will be covered with red plastic caps.

2. Positive terminals are bigger in size than negative terminals.

3. Positive terminals are marked + and negative terminals as −

4. Positive terminals are dark greyish in color and negative terminals are polished lead.

In all batteries a magic eye is provided, by opening the hood and looking at the magic eye on the top of battery if green color is visible the battery is fully charged. If yellow color is visible, it needs to be charged. If red is visible battery is discharged. Immediate correction or replacement is required. This is a very simple test, which can be done by the owner or driver.

In early days, the negative plates were wearing out in 2 to 3 months and batteries were replaced within 3 months. Now a battery's average life is anything between 3 and 4 years. By proper care, life of battery can be considerably increased.

The battery has to produce up to **100-ampere** current for operating self-starter and also help in producing up to **30000 volts** for spark ignition. It has to operate in all weather conditions. Now most of the batteries are called All Terrain Batteries (ATB).

The best help you can give to the battery is not to operate the self-starter for more than 15 seconds continuously. Because of continuous discharge of heavy current, (100 Amps) battery will not be able to produce the required current. The best method is to switch off ignition switch and wait for few minutes to enable the battery to recoup. Repeated or continuous operation of self-starter will seriously – affect battery life.

If your vehicle requires repeated cranking, get it checked immediately.

- Overcharging, This severely corrodes the positive plates, reduces battery life.

- Under charging, this will result in sulphation (formation of greenish deposits of lumps inside the battery) and results in short circuiting.

- Leaving battery idle – this will cause battery to run down to self-discharge, as inaction causes formation of sulphates and reduce battery life.

- High specific gravity: Concentrated Electrolyte. This is destructive and **will reduce battery life.**

- Impure topping up of water. Impure non-distilled water introduces impurities, which accumulates with each topping. In new generation batteries this is almost eliminated.

- Neglect to top up. This leads to exposure of portion of the plates, because of reduced level of electrolyte. The exposed position becomes hard and dry and losses capacity.

- Container damage: mishandling or dropping the battery causes this. Too tight or extremely loose clamps will result in cracks due to vibration.

Some points to remember:

a. Driving a vehicle will not always recharge the battery fully.

b. A battery will loose its charge on storage.

c. Maintenance free battery also requires topping up.

d. Never add acid to a battery in service. Add only distilled water.

e. Battery may explode due to short-circuiting.

f. Never test alternator by disconnecting the battery.

g. Avoid over and under charging. But keep battery fully charged.

h. Never try to start the vehicle by towing or push start. This will damage the hollow camshaft of the engine. You are taking the risk of loosing warranty, because of wrong use.

Hazards Related to Battery

Battery contains lead, sulphuric acid. The acid is corrosive when it spills over the automobile parts or on your body; it corrodes the parts and causes serious irritation to the skin. If acid falls on eyes it can seriously impair vision. Keep the battery spill proof. In case of spilling wash it down with plenty of water and immediately contact doctor for necessary medical assistance. Pure sulphuric acid is extremely harmful.

Electrical hazards because of sparking in case of short circuit or loose contacts. In case of gasoline (petrol) engines it is extremely dangerous and may cause fire and explosion.

Extreme short circuit will cause sudden heavy discharge and battery may explode. To avoid getting stranded it is necessary to keep the battery and electrical system in perfect condition. It will also prevent avoidable failures of electrical components.

Some of the future possible developments in automotive electrical components are:

1. Electrical cars totally or partially run on electricity. This is a totally different concept.

2. Because of increased electrical loads future systems will be operating on 42 volts (3–12 volts and one 6 volts battery). USA, Germany, Japan has already developed this system. In India companies like LUCAS – TVS are already developing 42 volts system to suit Indian conditions.

3. Electronics will control most of the functions in future. This will improve accuracy and speed and reduce the number of components. It is estimated more than 2000 components will be reduced in the vehicles due to introduction of electronic controls.

4. Fewer maintenance problems as electronic items will have longer life because of their hermitically sealed compact design and no moving parts and they are all static by the nature of their design.

Future electric vehicles will be fitted with LITHIUM-Ion batteries instead of lead acid batteries. They store more energy in smaller space than lead acid batteries.

Compared to lead acid batteries lithium-ion batteries store.

A. By weight: Holds three times more energy and provides 15 times more power

B. By volume: Holds 2 times more energy and provides 10 times more power

Presently high cost is the main hurdle for introducing Lithium-ion batteries, Once this problem is overcome we will find more and more vehicles with LITHIUM-ION batteries.

From owner/driver's point of view and safety, reliability, proper maintenance of electrical system is absolutely essential. It consists of simple, periodical checks, costing negligible amount. All systems in the vehicle are directly or indirectly connected through the electric system.

The other important electrical systems in the automobile are

a. Charging system: This consists of an alternator, producing necessary alternating current, which is converted into directed current by rectifiers. A belt drives it from engine. The belt tension and charging rate must be checked for correctness. Loose belt will cause slipping, which will reduce charging; too tight a belt will result in serious damage by overheating and failure of the alternator. This system requires little or no maintenance except for checking fan belts and timely replacement. But mishandling for example removing battery terminal when engine is running or doing any electric welding work without disconnecting both the battery terminals can ruin even a brand new alternator.

Lights and other accessories: Most of the lights and other controls like central locking, power windows, horns, wind shield wipers etc, take up considerable electric load. Use then with prudence and care. Guard against possible short circuits anywhere. Do not depend on fuses always.

Air conditioning systems: All future cars will have air conditioning and climate control systems as standard fitment. A lot of safety features is built in the ac system. Carefully go through all manufacturers' instructions and follow them, Mind your a/c system consumes substantial engine power and have an electrical load of up to 30–35 amps.

Electronic control module or on board computer: All engine controls like multi point fuel injection, antilock brakes, radars, lane departure warning system, sleep warning systems, night visions, air bag, emission control systems are controlled electronically. In the car high-powered sensors are fitted in various strategic locations. They provide necessary inputs to the computer, which in turn controls various systems, warn, drivers in advance. The ECM ensures self correction of the affected systems. They serve admirably without any maintenance attention so long as their input voltages are stable.

They are all extremely sensitive components, and even a very small defect in the electrical system can cause serious damage and mal functioning of systems.

Safety Features: Systems like air bags, night vision radar, ABS warning systems, collision avoidance systems, crumple zones are activated in case of emergencies. They are not required for normal running. They are also controlled by extremely sensitive sensors fitted in various locations and can act within milliseconds.

Regular checking is required. Special instruments, which must be connected to on board computers, can check these systems. This will indicate defects in the system much before they occur, so that corrections can be made. There are malfunction indicators, which will pin point the defective system.

Owners and drivers must also have a thorough knowledge about all controls and instruments and should be able to know the various codes of malfunction indicators. Their role is increasing day by day. Repeated reading of owner's manual and keeping them about the latest modification are part of the driving.

Future drivers will have to develop knowledge, skill and sharpness to changes at all times. Importance of knowledge cannot be slighted nor taken lightly.

Power Unit

This is where the power to run the vehicle is produced. This may be a conventional engine, alternatively fuelled engine, electric motors, and fuel cell vehicles. This is also a major source of pollution.

At present more than 99% of vehicles are having internal combustion engine, (IC engines). In this fuel and air mixture is burnt inside the engine and power is produced.

To understand the working of IC engine it is necessary to learn a few fundamentals.

The burning of fuel is known as combustion. For burning four essential elements are required. Fuel, air, space and mode for ignition.

Facts about Combustion

- Gasoline (Petrol) weighs approximately 600 times as air at sea level.

- Air required for burning is about 15 times, of fuel by weight, this is called air fuel ratio: 15:1. For burning 1 cubic feet of fuel we need 9000 cubic feet of air.

- Air is composed of 78 percent nitrogen, 20 percent oxygen (this is required for burning) and 2 percent other gases.

- When 1009 cubic feet of air weighing 80 lbs (approx) and 1 gallon of petrol weighing 6 lbs go into the engine about 968.62 cubic feet of exhaust gases (pollution) come out of the exhaust system out of tail pipe. It contains

Water	–	7.74 lbs
Carbon dioxide (Co_2)	–	13.78 lbs
Carbon Monoxide (Co)	–	3.27 lbs
Hydrogen (H_2)	–	0.993 lbs
Oxygen	–	None (ideal)
Nitrogen	–	62.08 lbs

In fact the most important requirement now is to reduce the pollution level and its ill effects.

Maximum temperature during combustion is 4500°F and combustion flame travels at a speed of 3000 feet/minute.

Even with a spectacular development in design, metallurgy, fuel and lubricants research and developments only about 35% of the energy available in fuel is converted into useful work. 5–10% goes as frictional resistance 30% goes out in heat taken by cooling and 30% goes out as exhaust gases.

The modern automobile engine is more than an engineering marvel. It contains components, which rotates at 150000 revolutions per minute. (Turbo charger shaft) and piston, which moves up and down with speed of 120 kilometer per hour, coming to abrupt stop 9000 times every minute.

The idea of giving information of this nature is to make the reader to realize the complex movements and other activities we demand from the automobile. It is similar to understanding functioning of our heart, lungs, brain etc. we naturally develop respect and treat them well.

Some of the main components of an internal combustion engine are given in the drawing.

It can be seen that the engine has many components that must work in harmony and rhythm. Now some of the terms used in automobile engines. They are common to all engines irrespective of fuel used.

For every revolution of crankshaft the piston moves up and down two times. Each movement is called a stroke. The engine, which completes its one activity in four strokes, or two revolutions of the crankshaft, is-called a Four-stroke engine. The working of four-stroke engine is given below.

First stroke is suction in which the air fuel mixture is drawn inside the cylinder during compression stroke the mixture is compressed and ignited by a spark in power stroke power is produced by the burning of air fuel mixture, which drives the engine. In exhaust stroke the burnt air fuel is expelled.

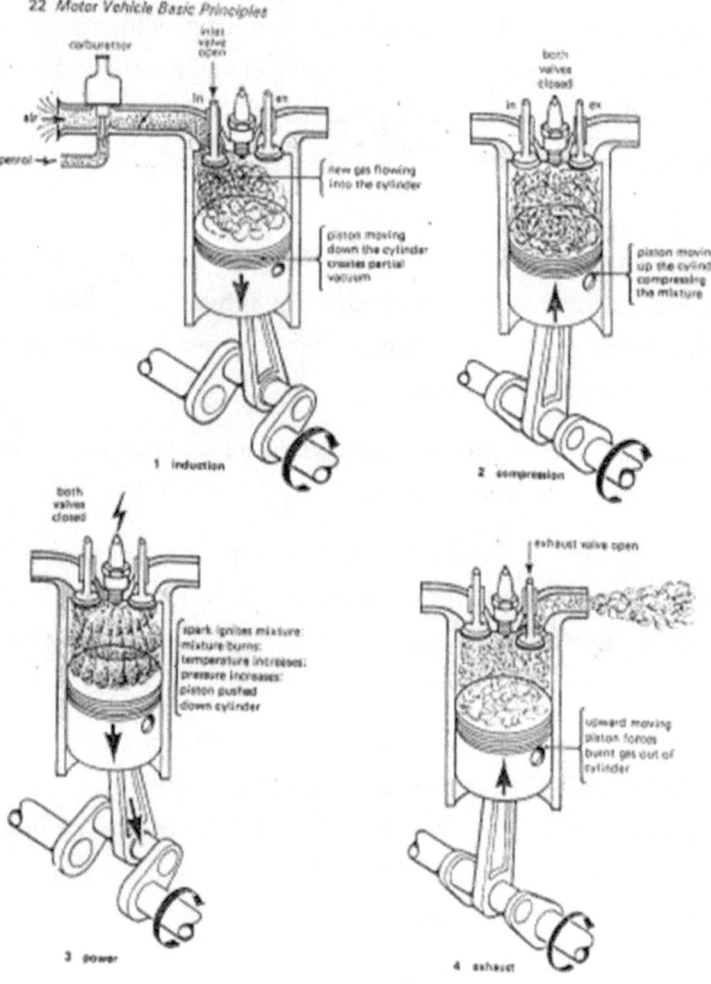

22 *Motor Vehicle Basic Principles*

Four-stroke operation

This cycle is repeated in the same sequence.

The basic principles of some improvements, which have taken place over period of time, are

a. Fuel – Instead of petrol diesel is used as fuel, and alternative fuels like LPU CNG Ethanol, are also used.

b. Injection of fuel by multiport fuel injection (MPFI) gasoline directs injection (GDI) common rail system and necessary modification for use of alternative fuels.

c. Ignition: Electronic ignition and computerized ignition, which are very accurate and senses even slightest changes in working conditions.

d. Fuels and oils: Lead free petrol's and low sulphur diesels, high performance lubricating oils are used for improving performance.

e. Catalytic converters: To transform harmful exhaust gases into harmless gases and to reduce pollution.

f. Metallurgical development in ferrous (Iron) Non ferrous (brass copper etc) and non metal (Plastics, rubber, fiber etc) to reduce weight and improve economy and safety.

g. Design of roads, bridges etc to reduce congestion, improve environment and overall economy in fuel consumption and reduce pollution.

Most of the present and future generation engine controls will be electronic. As long as the driver is keeping the electrical system in general and the battery in particular, in good condition, the vehicles will not give any problem. Even if some defects develop they will be indicated as malfunction indicators.

Normally the malfunction indicators, will show once followed by few blinks. First one indicates 10 followed by number of blinks. The details about Maruthi vehicles are given as example. Every manufacturer has their own indicator code. They are given in owner's manual.

The location, function and indication will vary from vehicle to vehicle. Above is given as a model only. For each type of vehicle owner's manual is to be referred and followed.

The diagnostic modes may vary for different vehicles. But it will be guidance for troubleshooting. Again manufacture's recommendations must only be followed.

Now, let us know about one of the important component of the engine-piston. The astonishing way the piston functions makes it the most important component of the vehicle.

The primary function of the piston is to receive the thrust generated by the explosion of gas in the cylinder during burning and transmit the force.

It also reciprocates in the cylinder as a gas tight plug to cause suction, compression, expansion and expulsions of burnt gases. It helps to convert the chemical energy in the fuel to useful mechanical power. The efficiency and economy of the engine primarily depends on the working of the piston.

It must operate in the cylinder with minimum of friction and should be able to withstand the high explosive force developed in the engine and also the very high temperature ranging from 2000 °C to over 2800 °C during operation, which is sufficient to melt any known metal. It should also give away the heat in shortest possible time.

The piston should be as strong as possible; its weight must be minimized as far as possible in order to reduce the inertia due to its reciprocating mass.

The present engines run at speed of 5000–6000 Revolutions per minute (RPM) and some engines run even up to 9500–10000 RPM. The mean piston speed for an average engine ranges from 2500–3500 feet per minute with about 9000 stops every minute, when the engine Revolves at 4500 RPM.

The picture of an automotive engine assembly indicating various parts and the piston and connecting rod assembly are given. Also the temperature inside the cylinder is given. This should give an idea of the various thermal and mechanical stresses acting on various components of the engine. Similarly other components are also subjected to tension, compression, and shear forces. It is really a wonder how these stresses are being managed.

Piston in the automobile is an important component and given as an example because of it's High stress, temperature, pressure, and its speed of movement. The purpose of this chapter is not to make an automobile engineer out of the reader. It is to make the reader understand the complex functions and how safe driving and proper and timely maintenance can enhance the vehicle reliability and safety.

Transmission system: Clutch to rear axle assembly. The gear assembly carries the power that the engine produces to the car wheels. It consists of clutch (in case of manual transmission) transmission (gearbox), drive shaft (propeller shaft) differential and wheel axles.

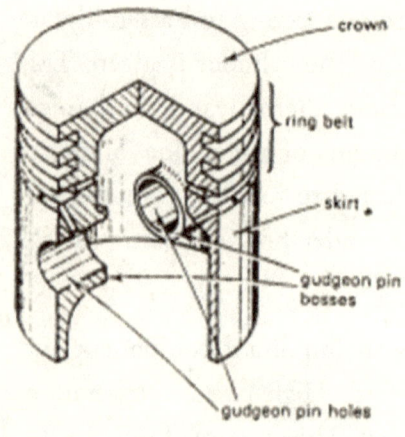
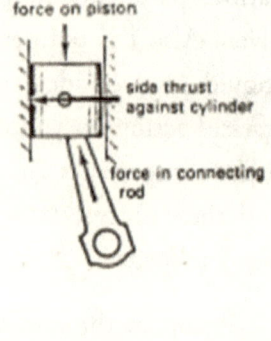

crown

ring belt

skirt

gudgeon pin bosses

gudgeon pin holes

force on piston

side thrust against cylinder

force in connecting rod

Main features of a piston

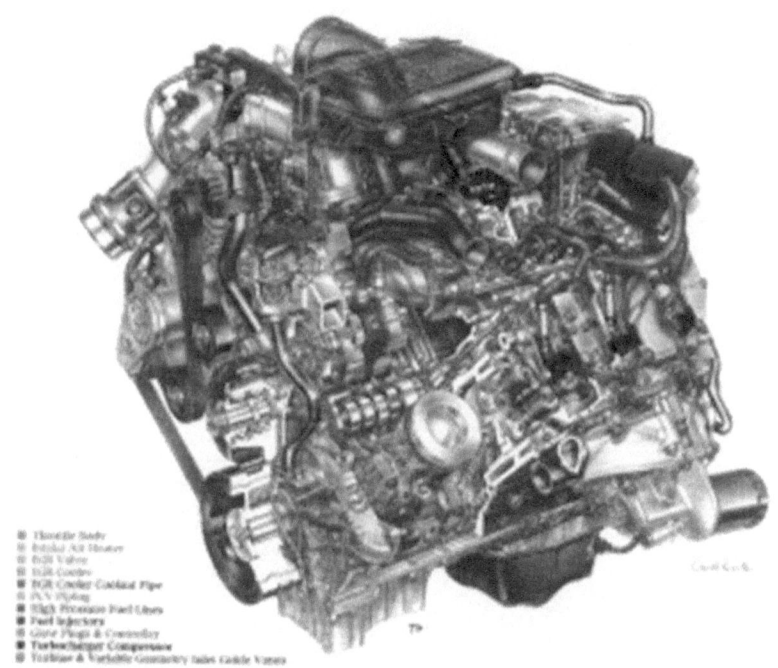

- Throttle Body
- Intake Air Heater
- EGR Valve
- EGR Cooler
- EGR Cooler Coolant Pipe
- PCV Piping
- High Pressure Fuel Lines
- Fuel Injectors
- Glow Plugs & Controller
- Turbocharger Compressor
- Turbine & Variable Geometry Inlet Guide Vanes

AUTOMOTIVE ENGINE ASSEMBLY

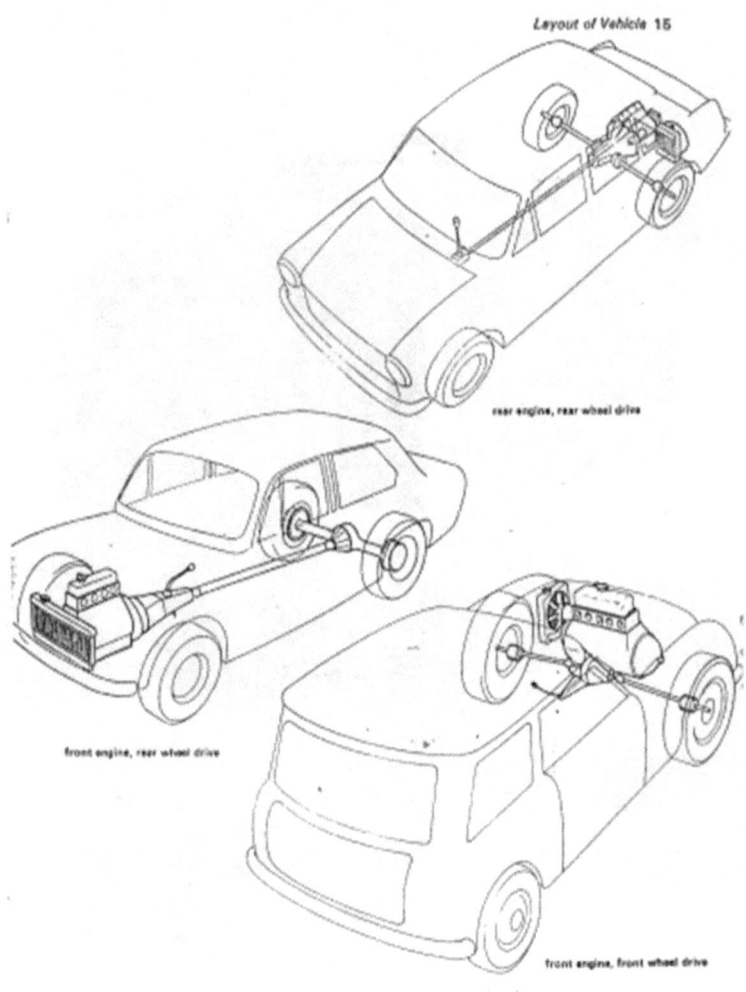

Layout of Vehicle 15

rear engine, rear wheel drive

front engine, rear wheel drive

front engine, front wheel drive

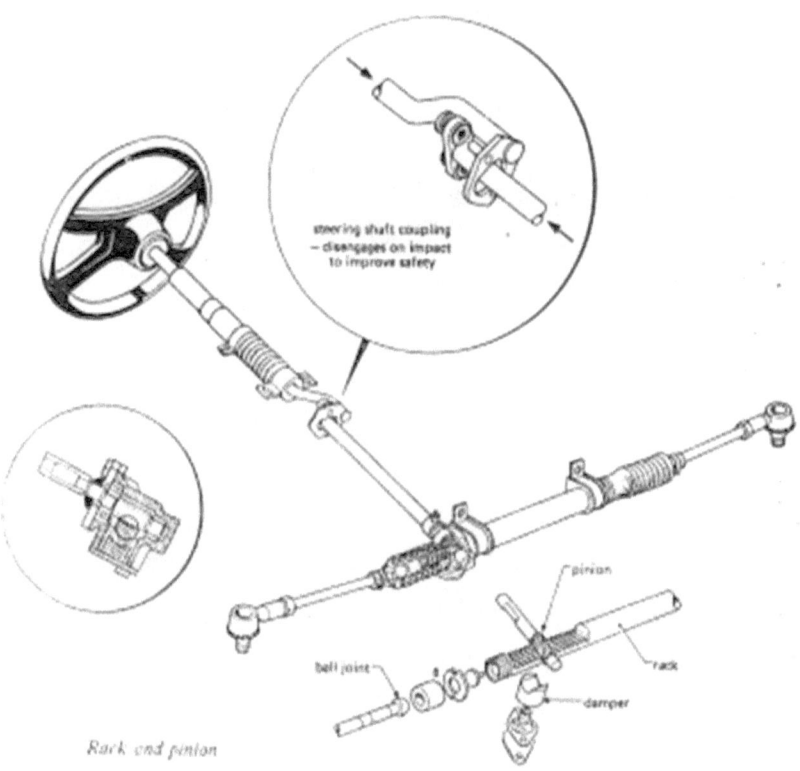

steering shaft coupling
– disengages on impact
to improve safety

pinion

ball joint

rack

damper

Rack and pinion

The purpose of clutch is to permit the driver to engage or disengage the engine and transmission. When the clutch is in normal running position (engaged) power flows through it from the engine to transmission. If the transmission is in gear, it flows on through to the car wheels so that the car moves. The transmission provides a means of altering the gear ratio between the engine and car wheels. The different gear ratios are necessary since the engine does not develop much power at low speeds.

Whenever we are making a turn, right, left or U turn, the inner wheel, of the curve should travel less distance than outer wheels. They form arcs of different diameter circles. This is achieved by differential unit, which permits outer wheel to rotate more than inner wheel in the same time.

There are basically four types of drives. They are:

1. Front engine rear wheel drive: The engine is in the front side and rear wheels are drive wheels.

2. Front engine front wheel drive: The engine and drive wheels are in front side. The engine is mounted across or transverse mounting.

3. Rear engine rear drive: The engine as well as drive wheels is in rear.

4. All wheel drive: The engine is in front and both front and rear wheels are drive wheels. This type is specially designed for all terrains.

Examples: Maruthi 800/Zen are front engine front wheel drives.

Maruthi Omni is front engine rear wheel drive. Maruthi Gypsy: Front engine all wheel drive.

Volks wagon Beetle (German) is rear engine rear wheel drive.

Steering System: All motor vehicles must have a steering control. Most of the cars have rack and pinion steering. It is simple in construction and has fewer linkages, which are of much advantage in operation. The same system can be operated by hydraulic power or electronic control. Most of future vehicles will be having electronic steering, which is highly sensitive and effective at all speeds.

Suspension: The method in which all wheels are attached to the frame is called suspension. Now most of the cars have all wheel independent suspension, which permit independent movement of all wheels with reference to each other. A novel and revolutionary suspension system is mentioned in chapter under the caption "Future cars." Present suspension systems are hydraulic, pneumatic (Air suspension).

Brakes: This system is the most essential, without a proper and efficient brake system all other developments will be of no use. All present and future generation vehicles will have an anti-lock braking system, which will control each wheel braking force as per ground requirement of each wheel. This will prevent most common malady in brakes, which produces skidding. When vehicles skid there can be no control of the vehicle either in steering or braking.

Coachwork or body: Now this assumes maximum importance, during selection of vehicles. It gives aesthetic look and style combined with aerodynamics. Major decision on buying is decided by the styling and appearance. Crores of rupees are spent in research and development in body design finish and painting.

Safety System: Pollution control and safety are two major aspects, which are going to be main criteria for design of future cars. Many safety features in accident avoidance reduce, the impact in the event of unfortunate accidents and advance-warning systems will become a part of future safety. Some of the safety systems are described in the future cars.

In an automobile all systems should work in coordination with each other. Any malfunction of one system will have an impact on many other systems. For example if the drive belt of alternator and water pump breaks, both cooling and charging system will be affected first. And as a consequence of this, electrical system will breakdown and overheating and even seizure of engine will be the result.

To ensure that all systems are working properly, the driver should exercise regular checks on various systems. Tips for prolonging the life of your car and increase its reliability and economy is given in a separate chapter. Following these tips will be of great help in safe and sane driving.

The purpose of including this chapter is to make the reader to know the functions of various systems and the stress and strains they are undergoing in normal running as well as the effects of improper care on various systems.

Once we are in tune with our vehicle we develop much more than man machine relationship. This will convert our vehicle into a reliable and trust worthy companion.

This you will find in all racing cars and their drivers. They become one integral component of the car during any car race.

* * * * *

Lawyer defending a client charged with drunken driving tells the Judge. Your honor, my client is a very sober person. When he is sober he is always against drunken driving.

* * * * *

A woman was hurrying home to convey good news to her family in her car. On her way home she dashed against three vehicles and hit a lamp-post before reaching home. The news she wanted to convey was she had been appointed as a driving instructor in a driving school.

* * * * *

Importance of Maintenance

Like the air we breath, the food we take and water we drink has tremendous effect on our health, clean fuel, air and lubricants we use are very important for vehicle life.

Maintaining a vehicle involve in physical contact with the vehicle. This will gradually develop into more intimate affinity to the machine.

The vehicle can be compared to a human body in many ways. One area of similarity is that of health and life span. Just as basic hygiene (washing hands, brushing and gargling etc.) help preventing diseases, daily vehicle care also helps the vehicles work in a trouble free manner.

Moreover just as we are responsible for our own health daily upkeep is the responsibility of the drivers/owners.

Just as the cost of the treatment and the time of recovery keep increasing as the disease progresses, so is also true with the vehicle. The cost of daily prevention and periodic checkup is minimal compared to expenses incurred when health care is neglected and when illness leads to hospitalization. The daily and periodical maintenance to the vehicle will contribute to effective vehicle performance.

Like the air we breathe and food we take has tremendous effect on our health, the clean air, fuel and lubricants are important for vehicle life.

Maintaining a vehicle involves three aspects cleaning, lubrication and bolting. Cleaning of the vehicle enables us to have better condition of the various parts and lubrication with proper recommended oils and grease will prolong the life and friction free performance. Proper bolting or ensuring tightness of various bolts and nuts (e.g. wheel nuts) will ensure safety in performance.

All these activities involve physical contact with the vehicle. This will gradually develop into more intimate relationship.

By this it is possible to know and rectify the defects much before and prevent damages. Even a single loose bolt can be the direct cause of failure and sometime may cause catastrophic damage.

Proper and timely maintenance will ensure vehicle reliability, safety in use, reduced running, maintenance costs. Above all it will give us the satisfaction of possessing an asset we can be proud of.

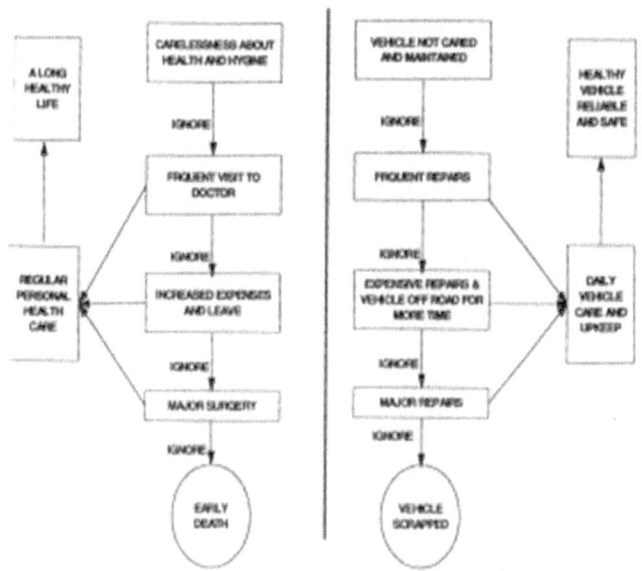

THE ABOVE CHART IS SELF EXPLANATORY COMPARISON OF MAN AND MACHINERY

Servicing and Repairs of Vehicles

Best recipe for trouble and accident free vehicle is a well Maintained vehicle and safe, sane and matured driver.

Whether new or pre owned cars or two wheelers, heavy or light vehicles, all of them must be periodically serviced, maintained, repaired as and when required.

All the above are required to maintain a safe vehicle. Best recipe for trouble and accident free vehicle is a well-maintained vehicle and safe and matured driver.

All present and future generation vehicles are manufactured with absolute precision and almost all components will be having a very long trouble free life.

At the same time carrying out any form of repair is a specialized job and requires special tools and diagnostic equipment and well-trained professionals with complexity of today's and tomorrow's machines the technical knowledge a mechanic must possess is staggering. For example Ford service manuals runs 420000 pages. It is really difficult to find and train a qualified mechanic.

Like what is required in the medical profession, repairing, servicing of modern automobiles is becoming more and more a specialized job.

EVOLUTION: Initially mechanic learnt from hard knocks, shimmied knuckles and bashed fingers. Secrets were hardly taught. In no other industry will you find such a blurred line of distinction between those who are really qualified and those who are not.

In India we are developing extremely fast with modern technologies, but we are not able to shed our love for old Ambassadors, Fiats, Vespas etc. Cycle rickshaws are plying side by side with Mercedes E220s.

Tests for engine repairs, performance, suspension, brakes, automatic transmission, axles, electrical, climate control systems, require special tools, gauges, and also the necessary skill to use them. They can be handled only by specially trained mechanics.

Factory dealership trained persons have access to latest diagnostic tools, attend frequent refresher courses and read technical bulletin and undergo pre product launch training etc.

It is necessary to know various facts associated with repairs

- Approximately 40% of the cost associated with auto repairs is unnecessary. This translates to about 40 billion dollars a year for about 181 million vehicles in US in INDIA we have over 60 million vehicles and we also face similar problem, may be to a lesser degree.

Main Reasons

- Lack of basic knowledge about – vehicle of the owners/customers.

- Unneeded parts thrust on you in a package deal.

- Unneeded repair due to faulty diagnosis.

- Faulty repairs for which no refund is made to the customer.

- Unneeded Repairs.

- Unnecessary preventive maintenance.

- Vehicle design requiring use of overly modularized parts.

- Highly non-standardized parts.

- Accidents due to faulty repairs.

- Waste fuel and oil.

All the above are findings in USA. In India condition may slightly differ, but some of the basic issues remain. In fact our repair problems are more complex because of plenty of old and new vehicles are plying side by side. Besides, we have a taste for re-conditioning of vehicles and hence a plethora of subsidiary workshops which concentrate only **re-conditioning** and not doing any original repair.

To quote famous Consumer Activist: RALPH NADAR. An ounce of mental prevention is worth a pound of dollar cure.

With the backdrop of the above scenario, it is necessary to have prudent selection of a proper repair agency. Let us analyze the issues for new vehicles first followed by pre-owned/ old vehicles. All new cars, two wheelers, other vehicle are manufactured and sold through their authorized dealers across the country.

You have the liberty to choose any car/model/color/ price/options etc and also choose the dealer for purchasing a vehicle. More about this given in 'buying a vehicle'

Each vehicle sold, carry warranties and other conditions of sale. Now a days most of the manufacturers give fairly good and long duration warranty for their vehicles. But all warranties carry **conditions.**

The declared warranty polices are available on request from all automobile manufacturers.

Certain relevant clauses are reproduced below:

Warranty Policy

(Manufacturers) warrants that each vehicle distributed in India by (manufactures) and sold by an authorized dealer will be free, under normal use and service, from any defects in material and workmanship subject to the following terms and conditions.

Qualification

To quality for this warranty

a. The vehicle must be set up, serviced and delivered by an authorized dealer.

b. Warranty registration card in respect of each vehicle, must be completed by the dealer and pre-delivery inspection done before delivery.

Warranty Obligation

If any defect(s) should be found in a vehicle within the terms stipulated, the only obligation is to repair or replace at its sole discretion any part shown to be defective with a new part or the equivalent at no cost to the owner for parts or labor, when they acknowledge that such a defect is attributable to faulty material or workmanship at the time of manufacture. The owner is responsible for any repair or replacements, which are not covered by this warranty.

Limitation

This Warranty shall not apply to

a. Normal maintenance other than free services including without limitation, oil and fluid changes, headlight aiming, fastener retightening, wheel balancing etc.

b. The replacement of normal wear parts including bulbs, battery tires and tubes, spark plug, brake lining, belts, hoses, filters, wiper blades, brushes. etc.

c. Vehicles used in competitive racing.

d. Any repairs or replacement required as a result of accident or collision.

e. Any defect caused by misuse/negligence, abnormal use or in sufficient cause.

f. Any modification not authorized.

g. Use of non-genuine spares or accessories.

h. Natural wear and tear for air condition system, V belts, hoses and gas leaks.

Extent

This warranty is the entire written warranty and nobody can extend or enlarge the warranty.

Disclaimer of consequential damage.

Missing Mechanic

Manufacturers assume no responsibility for loss of vehicle, loss of time, inconvenience or any other indirect, incidental or consequential damage resulting from the vehicle not being available to the owner because of any defect covered by this warranty.

The above are given so that the owner realizes the importance and necessity to have a valid warranty.

Analyze thoroughly and select a dealer who will hold the warranty in letter and sprit. This may require your traveling more distance and spend more time. It is worth the effort.

Awell-maintained vehicle will be an asset to any dealer. He/she will walk an extra mile to retain customers like you and offer special incentives. You can expect excellent after-sales service. A good reputed dealer can form an effective link between owners and manufactures and raise customer satisfaction index.

Customer satisfaction can be turned into customer delight.

Pre Owned/Old Vehicles

Nowadays, a lot of used vehicle dealers offer conditional warranty for vehicles sold by them. Whether new or old vehicles emission control is a must. All new vehicles carry emission warranty subject to the stipulation that none of the connecting system will be tampered. But even putting adulterated fuel will raise emission level above accepted limits. Future control is going to be more and more stringent. Running polluting vehicles may be banned in most of the places.

New or old, selection of reliable agency for servicing and repair is imperative from the user's point of view.

For all new cars under warranty, select the best dealer who is scrupulous in dealings and develop best inter-personal relationship with them. Good dealers can be of great help.

In the highly competitive automobile market dealers will always strive for better and lasting customer relationship. Most of the new car owners will be replacing the existing vehicles in 3 to 4 years. This psychology will be the prime factor in dealer-customer relationship.

While selecting repair/servicing agencies for pre-owned/old vehicles check:-

- The type of cars being repaired by the workshop.

- What facilities are available for carrying out necessary repairs.

- What kind of diagnostic tools and gauges they have.

- What repair guarantee do they give?

- How does their labor/spares cost compare with similar shops in your area.? Check at least two or three to make sure.

- Are they explicit in their dealings or withholding information?

In spite of all never develop affinity to any one. Always look for new places, get information from friend, experience and use them to your advantage.

Never allow yourself to be taken for a ride. Let there not be any room for you to feel that you could have still explored a few more.

Ideal Consumer Behavior

1. Respect yourself, maintain it.

2. Know what you want.

3. When mentioning about problem tell the workshop the symptoms and effects. Do not try to diagnose the defect yourself.

4. Be flexible to select workshop – whether dealer or any other workshop. So is the case with new or old car – make a thorough enquiry before making the buy.

5. Insist on getting your version in writing (symptoms) and be specific in asking for the copy of the work order and an authentic estimate for repairs duly signed by a regular authority.

6. Give specific instructions to workshop in charge not to carry out repairs not mentioned in the work order without your specific permission and approval of increased cost after estimation.

7. Ask for all old replaced parts and the workshop dealer must explain why the parts had to be replaced.

8. Do not respond in anger. Be always polite but firm.

9. Be ready for a battle if necessary but let it be the last course.

10. Lodge your grievances in writing.

    Complaint letter should be:

    A. laconic and specific.

    B.   Keep paras short and to the point.

    C.   Never sacrifice respect at any point nor indulging in foul language or threatening words.

Para 1: Product.

Para 2: Problem.

Para 3: Promises made by dealers/Manufacturers.

Para 4: What you now ask for as you find situation a strict variance from the promise.

Get proper acknowledgement for your letters and if dealer takes no action within the reasonable time given by you, raise your level of action.

No manufacturer or dealer can afford to ignore a genuine complaint of a customer for the simple reason that an aggrieved customer is a potential threat to the future of the company.

Some More Facts about Manufacturing of Automobiles

All the manufactures of various types of vehicles have obtained International certifications for quality. Likewise automobile ancillaries and raw material suppliers are also bound to have International quality approval. In the field of fuel and lubricants, construction of Roads/safety norms we are aiming at world-class qualities.

The work forces in automobile industry are among the highest paid. In UK it is a fact that a skilled automobile technician, who can handle latest electronic diagnostic gadgets gets paid much more than a successful doctor.

It is said in USA, automobile industry (manufacturers) work for 5 days a week Monday through Friday. They are paid on Fridays. It is a common practice to see the workers planning their weekends from Friday mornings. It normally extends up to Monday. Heavy absenteeism is on Monday, Tuesdays and lack of attention on Fridays. So only cars produced on Wednesday are likely to have the best quality control. This might have been mentioned in lighter vein, but there must be some element of truth in it. In India conditions are not like USA. Average control is better.

In spite of all quality controls sometimes defects occur due to any one or more factors.

Whenever such defects are noticed, the manufacturers themselves notify the dealers and rectify the defect on all affected models free of cost. This service extends beyond normal warranties given by company. This information is posted in company's website, dealer newsletters and consumer magazines.

It will be a good practice to know this information about the vehicle you are having.

Due to the heavy competition, manufacturers of automobiles are revising their warranty policies regularly.

We should keep our selves well informed about the latest developments.

And use them to our advantage.

Spurious Spares

You will be surprised to know that almost every second part being sold in the market is spurious. Adulteration of fuels and lubricants compounds the problem of spurious spares.

The spurious spares is thriving as an Industry mainly because

- The original equipment manufacturers and auto component manufacturers are not able to meet the customer requirement fully.

- Millions of independent individual consumers lack technical knowledge and time.

- They are by and large substandard, and do not meet the industry specifications. Obviously they are cheaper.

- Many buyers do not understand the basic, that a product can be duplicated, but the quality cannot be duplicated and believe in the quality of the spurious spares.

- It is very difficult to identify spurious parts by visual inspection alone.

- The spurious spares have a very large market base, created by organized clandestine vendors. Just for example, the spurious segment of the Medicine market of our country has an investment running into crores.

- It creates an illusion of cost effectiveness. They work on the principle more work, more worry, no work, and no worry. For example fake filters are made of inferior grade paper and just give a look-alike appearance.

They do not function at all. They do not filter any impurities. So it lasts much longer than original filters. But the after effects are much more damaging and result in very costly repairs sometimes leading the owner to even scrapping of valuable assemblies.

How do the spurious spares reach the markets?

Worn out parts used by various fleet operators, garages and discarded vehicles are the main sources for the reconditioning industry. It is possible to get a reconditioned part for any vehicle in certain markets specializing in this. Here at least you are fully conscious that you are buying a reconditioned part.

Whatever is the method or process of reconditioning it can never equal the original items in quality and reliability. Everything has a price, after all. 'Quality can never be an accident' as Mahatma said. Let us understand these truisms.

The other avenue is clandestine manufacturing by unauthorized persons, who duplicate the part, but not the quality and dump them in open market. The cartons in which the parts are packed look very similar to the original manufacturers packing.

Since these items are readily available at comparatively cheaper rates, it has a very wide market base.

How to avoid the menace of spurious spares.

- The manufacturers of vehicles, auto ancillaries should educate the common man in a systematic manner, the evil effects of use of spurious spares. It is similar to use of spurious medicines. The effects can be catastrophic in damage, which may occur without any previous warning.

- To avoid illegal reconditioning and packing in original containers tamper proof containers may be used.

- Use two or three-dimensional holograms which cannot be duplicated.

- The government should encourage auto ancillary manufactures to produce spares in very large numbers and widen their market base, so that quality products are made available at competitive rates. This will reduce use of spurious spares.

- At present almost every second part sold in market is a spurious spare.

- Effects of spurious spares.

- Loss of revenue to Govt. due to tax evasion.

- High number of Accidents due to poor performance of safety related components.

- Reduced fuel efficiency.

- Shorter life span of spares.

- Increased pollution due to adulterated fuels and fuel injection spares.

- Seriously impairs functioning of affected components like a rotten apple in an apple basket.

- Strict legal action is difficult as selling spurious spares is not a cognizable offence.

Critical parts like brakes, clutches, gears and fasteners; hoses safety glasses etc. are not ornamental fittings. With them you cannot and should not take a chance. You may be risking your own life and that of others by using spurious critical parts.

As the owner of any form of automobile you can help in reducing the menace of spurious spares by

- Getting your vehicle repaired/serviced in authorized service station. You can insist on the use of only genuine parts and ask them to confirm in writing.

- Never buy fuel and lubricants from unauthorized source. They may be adulterated.

- Drive cautiously and avoid unnecessary wear of spares. You will automatically reduce your repair bills.

- Keep yourself updated in use of spurious spares and their effects and learn how to avoid buying them.

Remember your own life and that of others is more valuable than the difference in cost between original genuine spares and spurious spare.

Tips for Prolonging the Life of Your Vehicles and Increase It's Reliability

Failure of cooling system had been identified as the prime cause of engine seizure and excessive wear of engine parts, which will lead to costly repair or replacement.

First of all you must remember, when you are driving a vehicle; many systems are working independently and in tandem with other systems. At any time more than 3000 parts are moving in relation to each other. The speed, types of movement are different from each other. For example the piston moves at a speed of 2000–3000 feet per minute. The turbochargers revolve at 1,50,000 revolutions per minute; the shock absorber may be moving few inches every minute, depending on road condition.

The owner/driver of any vehicle can carry out various checks on each system, before starting the journey, while driving the vehicle and at the end of the journey/day.

Engine

Normal points to be checked by driver or owner are:

a. Engine oil level. This is checked by a dipstick, which will have two level indicators max, and minimum. The level should be maintained near maximum limit. Too much oil is as bad as too little oil.

Only correct grade of lubricant and correct quantity must be used. Replacement of lubricating oil and oil filter as per recommended frequency is a must. During circulation the engine oil is under pressure, built by oil pump. All machined parts in the vehicle will have some working clearance between them. A thin film of oil must be maintained between bearings and shaft to prevent metal-to-metal contact.

Coolant Level

About 30% of heat generated in the engine is to be taken away by the cooling system. The engine should be running within the range of working temperature. Both overheating and over cooling are very bad for the engine. The coolant quantity and quality should be correct. Failure of cooling system has been identified as one of the prime causes of Engine seizure and excessive wear of engine parts.

All modern vehicles have coolant Element, ethylene glycol mixed with water, and sold as ready-mix coolant. Only good quality coolant to be used and correct level to be checked at least once in a week and add only coolant.

The normal working temperature is indicated in the temperature gauge generally by green shade. As soon as the engine is started the temperature should reach the desired range and should remain in the range throughout. The engine may be overheated due to

* Insufficient and incorrect coolant

* Broken or loose water pump drive belt

* Defective fan motor switch or relay

The vehicle should not be used in overheated condition. It may cause engine seizure and expensive avoidable repairs. Sometimes the damage caused may not be realized immediately. It will reduce engine life considerably.

Sometimes it may even happen. Due to overheating the engine may seize and come to an abrupt stop. It is most important not to get panicky and do something wrong. What happens is the following:

➢ Considerable coolant may be lost.

➢ All components inside the engine are overheated beyond permissible limit and there is no working clearance between pistons, cylinder, resulting in seizure.

➢ The whole cooling system will be in boiling state.

Be calm and proceed as follows:

➢ Park the vehicle in one extreme side of the road and be free from on-going traffic and get help to do this by pushing only.

➢ Open the bonnet; you will see lots of fumes all around. Leave the bonnet open and allow natural air to flow freely.

➢ Do not repeat Do not try to open radiator cap or coolant tank cap. It is boiling and you will get third degree burns if you come into contact with it.

➢ Now mind you, all components – particularly the piston are angry with you because of your negligence.

➢ But it is a very good product. It will cool down in the same way as it boiled. So patiently wait for about 30 minutes.

Now the most important operation starts.

It will be a good practice to have one litre of coolant, one litre of engine oil, and 250m1 of brake fluid at all times.

> "Take a thick cloth or a thick hand towel and slowly open the radiator cap. Lot of coolant may still spill out and it will be hot, make sure none of your body comes into contact. Turn your face away from radiator.

> Leave the cap open and allow fumes to escape.

> Now both the engine and you would have cooled down.

> In case coolant is not readily available. Plain warm water only should be used. Never use cold water!.

> Crank the engine. The engine may crank slowly. Do not crank for more than 5 seconds and repeat this few times. The engine will start. Do not accelerate. Allow the engine to run at slow speed and now slowly add coolant as warm water. Let it circulate gradually the engine will start running normally.

By having patience and following the procedure given above you can save the engine. Instead of this if you pour normal or cold water in a hot engine, components like cylinder-head, block may develop hairline cracks, because they are suddenly cooled from a very hot state. This is more with aluminum cylinder heads and blocks used in most of the vehicles.

Filters

There are three types of filters. Air cleaner element, oil filter and fuel filters. In this only Air Cleaner filter can be cleaned, other two filters are to be replaced. The air filter is one dry element type and highly efficient.

It is better to get these services done by professional people equipped and trained for doing the work. Particularly fuel system in present vehicles are electrically operated pressure systems. Extreme care must be taken to avoid any hazard in handling gasoline, which is highly inflammable.

Cleaning of air filter and replacing it at recommended frequency and replacing engine oil and fuel filters in time will ensure engines breathe clear air and supplied with clean and filtered oil and fuel. Never use non-genuine spares, as they will cause more damage and they are not environment friendly.

Exhaust System

The exhaust system of exhaust manifold, exhaust pipe, catalytic converter and tail pipe must allow free and uninterrupted flow of burnt gases. The main part is the catalytic converter, which converts the poisonous gases into harmless gas and water.

The only help it needs from you is filling of unadulterated, unleaded petrol. In future only unleaded, or further improved version only will be sold. But we cannot take guarantee on adulteration. It may continue.

Catalytic converter has numerous passages made of palladium or rhodium or platinum. When they are straightened out they will cover almost half a football field. This should give an idea of purification done by the unit. If the engine is in good condition, you cannot see any smoke and will hear only purring sound of the exhaust gas. The catalytic converter and other parts of exhaust system, will be in very hot condition after running. No attempt should be made to do any work in exhaust system when it is hot. You may get third degree burns.

Engine Mounts

The engine is mounted on the chassis or frame by flexible rubber mounting, to prevent engine vibration to chassis and road vibration to engine. Now most vehicles will have a hydraulic mount, which are self-adjusting and will safeguard from vibration and even create an electronic impulse to counter engine vibration.

Opening the bonnet we can check the condition of the mounts by holding the engine with both hands and slightly rock the engine. Any damaged mounts can be easily identified. Broken mounts will cause excessive vibration during running.

While checking and topping up coolant & oils, it is better to check level of wind shield water tank also and top up with clear water. Once in a year before onset of monsoon, replace all wiper blades. This will facilitate clear vision during rains and save windshield glass from scratches.

For proper and safe running of vehicle, the owner/driver must have some knowledge about various clearances, adjustments and checks.

Clutch

At present most of the vehicles are fitted with conventional clutch and normal transmission (gearbox). The clutch system comprises of the friction disc, which transmits the power. The friction linings are bound to wear out. The clutch is normally in engaged condition. When we depress the clutch pedal, we disengage the system.

One main defective driving habit is riding the clutch or keeping one foot on the clutch pedal while driving. We are partially disengaging the clutch, which is not desirable. This will result in uneven wear, Remember this type of wear is not governed under warranty and will involve very expensive repair.

The clutch during normal operation will have certain free movement of pedal called clutch free play. This free play reduces, as there is wear in the system. It has to be adjusted. The free play is measured in clutch pedal movement and normally around 20–25mm. Maintaining this is very important for smooth driving and prolonging life of clutch components. In automatic transmission this system is not required.

Steering Wheel Free Play

The steering wheel free play means movement of steering wheel without actually turning front wheels. This is measured as angular movement of steering wheel in degrees (normally it is around 30°). If it is more it indicates wear or loose linkage, and if it is less, too tight steering. Both are not desirable.

Brake Pedal Free play; A well maintained brake system will not interfere with normal running of the vehicle, but must come into action immediately on pressing the pedal. Providing recommended free play for the brake pedal would ensure this. Normally the brake and clutch pedal should be at the same level. Normal brake pedal free play will be around 25–30mm. Unlike wear in clutch, brake linings wear only when brakes are applied. As the wear increase the free play increases. In both clutch and brakes there is wear limit; if wear exceeds the limit the clutch disc and brake linings must be replaced.

In present and future vehicles the brake system used is vacuum assisted, (anti skid lock hydraulic brake system). This reduces the drivers effort and also ensures the required braking effort is available in each wheel, depending on ground conditions and contact area of each wheel to the road surface. It prevents the most serious condition known as skidding, in which the vehicle will be simply dragged along the Road, as the wheels will remain locked.

The main point of uncertainty in use of brakes is that you do not know or can anticipate in advance, your emergent requirement. Under normal driving like when you approach a signal, intersection or destination, you can anticipate well in advance your braking requirement.

Keeping the brake system in absolutely reliable condition needs no over-emphasis. In vehicle brake fluid level warning lights, hand brakes on indication are provided to warn the driver. In addition to intelligent and anticipated use, keeping the brakes in fully dependable condition will be a major breakthrough in safe and sane driving.

It will be of interest to know the anatomy of braking process.

The usual aim when applying brakes of a vehicle is to stop safely. In actual practice in most cases, WHEN to apply brakes cannot be anticipated. It requires total undivided attention, and sense of anticipation on the part of the driver, during all moments of driving.

Number of factors like vehicle, tires, road, weather, driver, hazards, type of braking system, friction etc influence what can be termed as SAFE BRAKING.

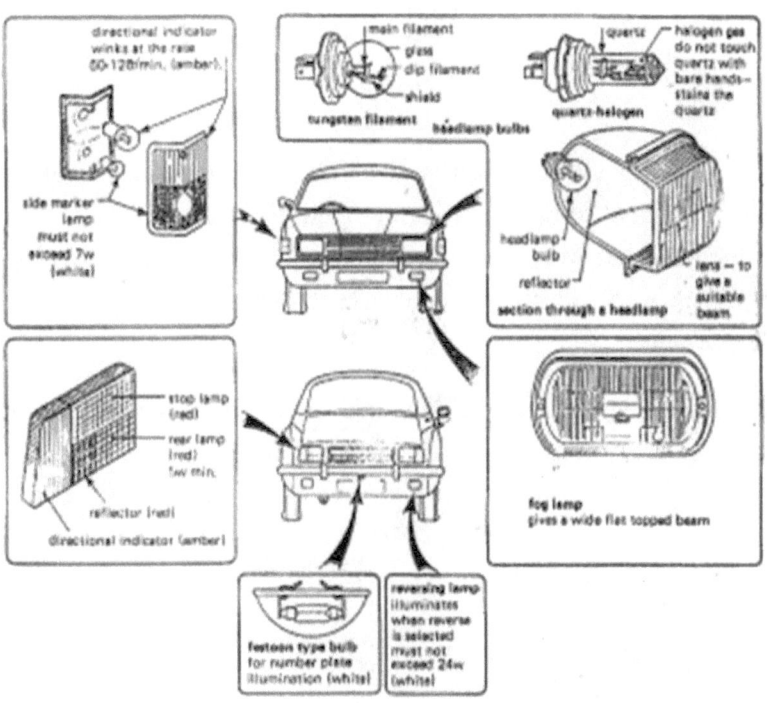

Lamp positions

Of all the factors DRIVER is the most important one.

An experienced, alert, healthy driver will react to a potentially hazardous situation and take required action. The reaction time includes recognition of the hazard, thought and movement of the right foot onto the brake pedal. It will be in the order of 0.5 second for a healthy, alert and experienced driver.

Any momentary lapse of the driver will increase this reaction time and will make all the difference between SAFE and UNSAFE braking.

The above illustration is given so that the reader becomes aware of the complex issues of braking. They should always remember that every moment of driving is important Maintaining the braking system in absolutely reliable condition is of utmost importance.

Handling emergencies like brake failure is given in a separate chapter listing possible emergencies. Every one must read and reread it a number of times.

Electrical Appliances

In the automobile every light is provided with some purpose. For our own safety and safety of all other road users, it is absolutely necessary to keep all lights in proper working condition, headlights in proper focused condition. Driving in night, light of other vehicles will mislead you about the speed and exact position. For example if only one head light is burning in vehicle coming in front, you can easily mistake the position and will realize the actual position only when the other vehicle is very near.

Similarly horns, wiper indications etc. are for safe driving and conveying our intention in an unmistakable manner. Driving in night without properly working electrical systems can be disastrous.

Tires

Besides being the costliest replacement item, tires form the only contact between the vehicle and the road.

Tires play an active role both in driving and stopping mode.

Maintaining tires is comparatively simple and cheap. To understand the importance of maintenance we must know certain basic principles.

Whether you use radial tire, normal tire or tubeless tire, it should be clearly understood that the air inside the tire plays an all-important role. It is the air inside the tire that takes the load, whether it is a bicycle or 100 Ton monster truck. The tires when in contact with the ground (road) exercise frictional contact, which is required while driving as well as braking, slowing down, and turning.

The automotive tires, care of a tire and tube or tubeless tire, wheel, on which it is mounted, and drum from where force for driving and braking is taken are all very important.

Every part of the tire has a specific function and this function will be ideal only when factors like tire pressure, load, speed, tread condition, balanced rims, alignment of wheels, tire rotation etc are properly checked and done in time and regularly.

Air is free !!!

Where the air has gone?

The owner can do most of the checks. Before starting the vehicle in the day, it is better to look at each tire including spare wheel for any unusual wear or change. If it is done daily even minor changes can be noticed., for these will affect tire wear and performance. For example, defective wheel alignment, worn or broken wheel bearing, or defective shock absorber can cause total failure of tire in a matter of hours.

Checking tire pressure costs practically nothing and will have lasting impact on tire life. At least once a week, check tire pressure in all wheels including spare wheel when tire is cold. (Early morning before using the vehicle). Always inflate to the recommended pressure only. Never over or under inflate, as both are injurious to tires.

Normally everybody talks about tire pressure. Very few will give importance to the quantity of air. Normal Air, which is surrounding us, is at certain pressure and temperature. This is called NTP (Normal Temperature and Pressure). In the same altitude pressure remains the same.

At sea level it is 14.7 lbs/sq inch or called as 1 bar. The temperature varies with season day and night, rain etc. Both pressure and temperature vary with altitudes. At higher altitudes pressure becomes less and that is why we have breathing problem at high altitudes and temperature will also becomes colder.

When we are inflating a tire we pump air inside the tube/tire. It is the quantity of air that builds up pressure. The air pumped inside will get compressed and pressure will increase. The pressure inside the tire is checked by tire pressure gauge and if it is more you pump out air and if it is less pump in more air.

As the vehicle run because of friction between tires and roads, heat is generated and the air inside the tire absorbs a portion of the heat and will have tendency to expand, since no space is available for expansion the pressure inside the tire increases. It is a temporary phenomenon and as soon as tire is cooled it will attain the original pressure. Earlier drivers particularly of commercial vehicles used to pump out the air, to reduce pressure. It is called bleeding. What they do not understand is they are reducing the quantity of air inside the tire. Which is very injurious and reduces tire life. It should never be done.

Remember it is the tread or outside portion, which is in contact with the ground, produces necessary friction during driving and braking. The tread depth is very important. If the tread is worn out it is called bald tire. Bald tire is extremely dangerous, as it will reduce the frictional force considerably and is a major cause of accident. 90% of tire related accidents are due to bald tires.

Present day tires are radial tires, puncture proof and have very long life. Owners/drivers can contribute a lot by proper and timely maintenance and check.

Future Tire Inflation

Presently all air craft tires are inflated by nitrogen instead of normal air. The same is being extended to automobiles in some parts of the world. We may be using it in the near future.

M/s. Ingersol Rand, Air Compressor manufacturers have developed nitrogen generators using membrane technology. This can be connected to any air compressor. Now more advanced technologies have come for generating nitrogen like candle generation etc.

Advantages of using nitrogen

* Tires run cooler

* Will not corrode the wheel

* Prevents under inflation

* Increases tire life

No moisture content as nitrogen is a dry inert gas

* Frequency of checking – the pressure is less, as there will be practically no air loss. In all cases the valve in the tire and valve cap must be in good and serviceable condition to prevent any leakage.

Tire Milage

Since the cost of replacement of tires is very high, proper selection and maintenance of tires are very important.

Even in the same model of vehicle, depending on the general usage proper tires must be selected. For example, vehicles used exclusively in cities in asphalted roads and similar vehicle used in hilly terrain of rough roads will require different types of tires.

It is preferable to change all the tires at the same time, or at least a pair of tires, so that uniformity is maintained.

Tires operate in all kinds of roads and conditions. Even minor variation for very short duration will have telling effect on tire life. Like under/over inflated tires, misalignment, or dragging brakes etc will damage the tire considerably and reduce tire life.

The following regular checks will increase the tire life considerably., and reduce maintenance cost

A. Check frequently at least once a week the tire pressure of all tires including spare tire when they are cold. (in NITROGEN filled tires this frequency of checking is reduced)

B. Rotate all the tires including spare wheel from front to rear and left to right This process will result in considerable increase in tire life and will also ensure uniformity of wear in all tires

C. Check daily before driving and at the end of the day for any unusual wear or slanting of tires

D. Select the proper size of tire, wheel rim depending on the general usage of the vehicle

By paying attention to minor details, which requires only time and practically at NO COST, you can achieve RELIABILITY, REDUCED MAINTAINENCE COST, RIDING COMFORT AND FEELING OF SAFETY.

As mentioned earlier, the purpose of chapters (How the automobile works' and 'Tips for prolonging the life of your car and increase its reliability) 1 are to impress the readers about the complex systems. Also to show that proper care and timely maintenance can have long lasting impact on vehicle, life and its reliability. It is absolutely essential for every driver/owner to read, understand and follow the instructions given by the manufactures, in 'Owner's Manual'and other literature.

I would like to quote two specific instances, in which the instructions given in the owner's manual were not followed and how it resulted in failure of vehicle prematurely.

First

The vehicle was Bedford J.5. Truck. This vehicle was fitted with CAV fuel system and Aglerometer. The fuel system is one of most efficient diesel fuel system and aglerometer is to filter water content in the fuel. The instructions are not to start the vehicle by towing as the fuel pumps are lubricated by diesel and if it runs dry without fuel, the pump will seize. The vehicle was started by towing. Immediately on starting, the fuel pump failed. And was to be replaced with a new pump. The cost of new pump was Rs. 20000.

Second

In the final drive differential was filled with special oil containing extreme pressure additives. It was to be replaced only after 7500 Km. But the oil was drained and normal final drive oil was filled after 1500 Km. The final drive crown wheel and pinion broke and replacement cost was Rs. 15,000/-.

Both failures occurred because of not reading, understanding and following the operator, manual and instructions.

With some basic training and knowledge all owners/drivers can carry out some checks periodically. This will prolong the life of the vehicle and ensure safety. One should take following precautions.

Safety Rules

1. Do not smoke or allow others nearby to smoke while working on your vehicle.

2. Never work without parking brake and gearshift in neutral.

3. Ensure the components are cold and do not attempt to remove it while the engine or other parts are hot.

4. Never Jack up the vehicle, unless wheels are properly blocked.

5. Use only insulated tools and wear proper dress and shoes/chappels while doing electrical work.

6. Use the wrench or spanner to loosen bolts carefully and pull the **wrenches towards you** rather pushing to avoid injury or bruised knuckles.

7. Take off your rings/wrist watches, long chain and other jewellery. Tie your hair, do not leave it loose, and never wear loose garments like loose duppattah or loose cloths.

8. While using toxic chemicals like anti freeze, coolant, electrolyte keep them away from your eyes and mouth and away from the reach for children and pets.

9. Gasoline (Petrol) is extremely dangerous because it is not only toxic and inflammable but vapor in the air in the empty can cause serious explosion.

10. Work in well ventilated area. Never work in closed room, garages while engine is running.

11. Keep the extinguisher handy in vehicle as well as in work place.

12. Handle all waste, rags with petrol, separately. Never mix with others.

13. Once in a month or after 1600 kilometers check the following. Check air filter. There are indicators in the Air cleaner assembly which will warn of choked' air cleaners.

14. Check the level of engine oil with the dipstick provided. It should be done when vehicle is parked on level ground and morning before starting the engine. Then only you will get correct reading. Add recommended grade of oil if required in correct quantity, and too much oil is equally bad as too little oil.

15. Check coolant level and quality and add only recommended coolant.

16. Check brake fluid level. This is very vital for safe braking.

17. Check windshield, wiper blades and washer liquid level.

18. Check automatic transmission fluid level.

19. Check drive belt for alternator water pump, power steering, AC compressor for unusual wear or glaze and. Get the needful done.

20. Walk around the vehicle to check tires and any leakage or unusual slanting of one side.

21. Check all controls, lights before moving.

Last but not the least never forget to put on seat belt before driving.

Most of the tips given in this chapter are easy to understand and follow. If done regularly it will take less time and will become a habit. The benefits you will be deriving will far exceed your efforts. You will be proud to posses an asset you can be rely on.

Pollution

There is a definite link between pollution caused by automobile exhaust and people's health. People's health definitely deteriorates under pollution effect.

All of us are in one way or other connected with pollution. Either we are the cause or sufferers or both of effects of pollution. As long as we have to breathe we have to suffer pollution effect. Automobiles have been identified and almost singled out as the main reason for pollution. We might actively produce pollution through our vehicles or passive sufferers when the vehicles on the road produce the pollution.

A small anecdote will give the insight of the issue.

'In 1273 AD an act of British parliament forbade burning of coal as it was beginning to choke the atmosphere. It was followed by a Royal proclamation by KING EDWARD I "whomsoever shall be found guilty of burning coal shall suffer the loss of his head."

Just imagine whether such a stringent law could be enacted today! The law was passed much before invention of automobiles.

There is a definite link between Air Pollution from Automobile exhaust and people's health. People's health definitely deteriorates under pollution.

More than 1/3 of the total vehicles are in metropolitan and other cities, which has only around 8% of the total population in India. This results in increased density of vehicles and increased pollution.

On an average a Motorist in cities inhale noxious gas equivalent to smoking about 10 packets of cigarettes every day. If you are a smoker or user of tobacco in any form add this to your daily consumption. (this may be appear to be an exaggeration, verify from experts on this field to satisfy your self).

Due to various constraints it is not possible to burn the fuel completely, so that no pollutions are thrown in exhaust. 100 years ago nobody thought of pollution as a problem. Now the whole world talks about green house effect, depletion of ozone layers and Kyoto convention etc.

Pollution control boards are working overtime. Whatever be the type of Road user you are, pollution is an issue for you.

All new vehicles, cars, commercial vehicles, two and three wheelers are comparable to the best in the world and meet international standards in pollution control. Over the year the pollution level had come down, which can be seen from following:-

Reduction	From	To	
Cars	16 gm/km	2.588/km	84%
Two Wheelers	20 gm/km	4.4598/km	80%
Trucks	35 gm/km	12.98/km	61%

But the number of vehicles and particularly two wheelers has increased to a very great extent offsetting the gains and so the gravity of the problem increases day by day.

In India an average driver uses vehicle for 9000 kilometers in a year. More than 33% of vehicles are concentrated in 23 cities having 8% of the population.

On an average a petrol car of medium engine capacity of 1200 cc and above produces 1 kg of carbon dioxide per every 12 kilometers of running. It is seen that new vehicles emit more pollution than old vehicles particularly SUVs of engine size of 3000 ccs of 1995–2000 models emitted 189 gms/km while 2005 and later models emit 256 gm/km… With increased number of SUVs total emission increased considerably… Average KPL is reduced from 14-km/liter to 10-km/liter in new model vehicles.

One of the major pollution causes is adulteration of fuel. In India we are able to produce only around 33 million tons of fuel against our requirement of 115 million tons of fuel. A very huge amount of 200000 crore rupees is spent for importing petroleum.

Cost of petrol and diesel are very high in India. That is the primary reason for adulteration. Mixing very harmful substances like Benzone, Taulane etc, results in harmful adulteration. Together they produce a very toxic exhaust.

Another major area in pollution is the fact that Indian vehicles in general are notoriously ill maintained. Even though vehicles are manufactured with very high accuracy and confirming to excellent pollution standards, bad maintenance and driving will offset all benefits.

In the science museum of St Louis, Missouri, USA, a vehicle is kept which will indicate the average pollution during different periods of time. We can operate the controls and from the exhaust gases we can learn pollution levels in Lbs of pollutions emitted by Average car/year.

1950	2006 lbs/year
1960	1788 lbs/year
1970	1417 lbs/year
1980	777 lbs/year
1990	549 lbs/year
2000	211 lbs/year

Reduction of 85% in 50 years/per vehicle/year

In India we have realized the importance of pollution control. Environmental protection is very high in our National Agenda.

Supreme Court in a landmark judgment on April 2, 1999, banned registration of private non commercial vehicles not confirming to euro 1 and 2 Norms. We cannot register any vehicles not conforming to euro norms in any of the major cities. Most of the states had passed laws on pollution control. Now Bharat stage 3/4/5 are in the offing, which corresponds to euro norms.

In diesel vehicles, peculiar problem of pollution known as particulates, which are extremely fine particles, which are coming out of exhaust. These particles are so fine, they cannot be filtered in normal exhaust system. They are very harmful to humans and animals alike. Once inhaled they form deposits in the lungs, and cause pulmonary diseases.

Enormous amounts are being spent in research, on how to cope up with this problem. Now specially designed particulate filters, which can filter up to 95% of the particulates, are being used in latest design vehicles. Specially designed catalytic converters are used to reduce the problem.

Selling diesel mixed with kerosene is the biggest pollution racket of the day. The revenue generated in this racket runs into about Rs. 24000 crores every year. Lots of vested interests are involved, and they would like to see this racket thrives. Adulteration thrives because no one wants to lose this income.

Their modus operandi is as follows

Kerosene costs around Rs. 9 per liter and diesel costs Rs. 36 as on May 2008. Mixing both in any proportion and selling it at a cheaper rate earns a tidy profit for the black marketers.

But kerosene contains as much as 2000 parts per million sulphur as against permissible 350 parts per million. So adulterated fuel not only damages the vehicle but also ruins people's health.

Only consolation is all people involved in adulteration racket also must breathe, the same air they are polluting. Knowingly they are causing irreparable damage to the environment and creating a new generation of unhealthy people.

We still have lot of scope in reducing pollution by switching over to alternative fuels. Some of them are LPG (Liquefied Petroleum Gas). This is a substitute petroleum product. Cost of conversion and running is quite high and it almost equals petrol. CNG (Compressed Natural Gas). Processing this is very difficult. The gas must be compressed up to 200 Atmospheric pressure. Storing such highly compressed gas requires special quality container, which adds to the weight and cost.

Both LPG and CNG are still not available for heavy commercial use.

Brazil is one country, which had done significant research in using Ethanol (basically taken as a by product of sugar cane industry). We have to make Herculean effort in this aspect. We have the capacity to produce around 300 billion liters of

Ethanol yearly. It will result in cost saving of Rs. 20000 crores every year. It should be the future objective of our country. But we should do the balancing act of producing ethanol without sacrificing the agricultural interests and creating famine.

Bio diesel extracted from Jetropha seeds (Kattu Amanakku) has similar properties of diesel and pollutes much less. Farming of Jetropha is being encouraged by states and Central Governments with buy-back options.

Field trails had been conducted in two most sophisticated vehicles (Mercedes Benz Viano C-220 computerized direct injected models. They were driven by pure bio diesel extracted form Jetropha seeds. They were taken from Delhi to Khardumgla (highest point in world's Highest Motor able Roads, in J&K. The performance was found to be satisfactory even in high altitudes (18060'above sea level).

Vehicles driven by Hydrogen fuel cells and electric cars are also in the run for pollution free environment. Reva the electric car manufacturer from Bangalore is already producing electric cars. Because of its limitation in use (100 Km with single charge) and less overall utility, it cannot be the only car in the family. As a second car with utility it is a choice.

Some of the main reasons for not achieving the desired standards of pollution control are:

- Our economic conditions do not permit scrapping of old vehicles completely. Still millions of the old vehicles are plying.

- Developments and use of alternative fuels is nowhere near our requirement.

- More than 60% vehicles in any city are two wheelers and they keep on increasing.

- IndianAutomobiles are normally ill maintained.

- Adulteration of fuel.

- Un regulated traffic.

- Absence of stringent laws on pollution control implementation.

- Totally unmanageable urban transport system.

The recent trend for indiscriminate licensing forAuto vehicles in Madras has indirectly brought down the fares all right; but with the same roads in ill maintained condition and lack of enforcement of traffic rules has compounded the problem for the user public. Almost similar trends exist all over the country.

The present fuel policy in any combination of fuel and vehicle leaves much to be desired, even though they may meet the prescribed emission norms as of now.

CNG is 30% cheaper and therefore the running cost use of CNG will reduce

CO (Carbon Monoxide) by 80%

NO (Nitrous oxide) by 50%

Ozone reactivity by 90%

Present cost of conversion:

CNG   Rs. 30–35000

LPG   Rs. 10–15000

Still we have to do a lot in implementing conversions.

A ill-maintained bus will emit 90 times more pollution than a well maintained bus carrying the same number of passengers for the same distance in the same route Both buses may of the same model and same year of production and same kilometers of running.

Governments, Non Government. Agencies, manufacturers of Automobiles have realized the importance of pollution control. They have taken several steps.

- Legal action against adulteration of fuels.

- Oil companies are now supplying lead free petrol and low sulphur diesel as fuels., the supplies are made in tamper proof containers, to prevent adulteration.

- Fitment of catalytic converter in all new cars from 1996.

- All new two wheelers to have only four stroke engines which cause less pollution.

- Pollution-under-Control certificate is mandatory for all vehicles.

- Amendment of motor vehicles acts permitting use of alternative fuels.

And many more steps are needed to educate and implement pollution control measures. Even though Automobiles manufactures, oil and fuel refineries and others had done excellent work to reduce pollution, our repair industry is nowhere near expectations. It has still not come under legal and technical standards, as there are no formal qualifications, experience, training specified to become a certified automobile repairer.

There are lots of things as vehicle owners, which we can do:-

- Do not buy fuels and oils from unauthorized sources.

- They will damage your vehicles as well as harm the environment.

- Regularly tune up the engine, If costs much less in the long run.

- Look for leaks.

- Keep tires properly inflated and regularly check the tire pressure.

- Look for leakage of Air Conditioner refrigerant.

- Use genuine oil, fuel and air filters and change them at recommended intervals.

- Use correct grades of oil, fuel for topping up and filling.

- Trust your senses.

- Drive at economical range of speed, preserve momentum and anticipate stops. The speed must be optimal always to save the fuel on one hand and reach the destination at reduced cost.

- Drive safely at all time.

- Plan and judiciously use vehicles.

You can contribute your mite in pollution control irrespective of what others are doing. You will be helping yourself, your family and society. Most important you will be doing a great service to future generations as well. We owe it to them.

Why vehicle pollution control is more important.

Industries can be relocated to shift pollution effect. But vehicles stay with settlement and people.

Whether you are a lawmaker or lawbreaker, or law-abiding citizen, you cannot escape the effects of pollution.

Whether you live in palace or hutment, pollution is a problem for you. Wherever there is air, it is mixed with pollution and hence universal.

In Delhi in 1993, 1500 people died in automobile accidents. In the same year 7500 people died because of pollution related diseases. Pollution kills more people than accidents. There is an urgent need to address both the problems on war footing.

As per recent findings by west coast center for oceans and human health (U.K), inhaling exhaust smoke from automobiles can cause Cardio Vascular disease or even Heart stroke.

The Polycyclic Aromatic Hydrocarbons found in fuels and oils can enter human blood stream and can affect heart's ability to pump blood effectively. In essence people living in urban areas are breathing an aerosolised oil spill. (fine form of spray).

Before concluding this chapter, Let us have a look at the latest report on pollution. In India during 2017, 12.4 lakh people died due to pollution related disease. In Delhi alone 12322 people died due to pollution.

77% of our population are exposed to Ambient Particulate matter PM 2.5.

It had overtaken deaths due to Tobacco consumption (10 lakh). Clear air is so rare, it is not available to any of us.

According to a world group study, global emissions of carbon Dioxide mainly from fossil fuels will increase by 2.7% in 2018. The fight against climate change is 'completely off course.'

Let us not get discouraged. Our renewed efforts with more vigour we will reduce the menace.

Let us hand over a better, environmentally pure world to our next generation, While reassuring a better atmosphere for the remaining period of our lives.

Handling Vehicle Emergencies

Emergency means sudden unforeseen event, which needs prompt attention. The problem with emergency is it comes without any announcement.

Responsibility of the drivers:

Driving a motor vehicle is a privilege and not a right. Everyone's safety is in driver's hands. Drivers have an obligation to society to do all that they can to prevent accidents. This means constant checking for possible troubles while driving. While you are on road, care of the vehicle is up to the driver and careless driving can cause accident at any speed. Take care of yourself, your vehicle, cargos, passengers, and pedestrian and motoring public.

The driver has a responsibility towards the other public, be they are vehicle drivers alike or pedestrians.

Even with all required skills, handling emergency is the most difficult. Emergency means sudden unforeseen thing or event needing prompt action. The problem with emergency is, it comes unannounced. If the drivers are alert and concentrating on driving at all times they can spot and act quickly in emergencies. Some of the emergencies, which can occur, and how best to handle them are given below.

Skidding

Handling skidding is the same for front and rear wheel driven vehicles.

Steps are given below.

1. Take your foot from the accelerator

2. But do not hit the brakes

3. Gently turn steering wheel in the direction of rear wheel skid

Be careful not to brake or turn sharply. Hitting the brake or jerking the steering wheel will only make the skid worse.

Driving in Fog

It is very dangerous to drive in foggy climate.

If you must:

1. You should slow down your speed.

2. Be alert and ready to stop.

3. Use fog lights if provided. They give yellow beam, which can penetrate fog, otherwise use low beam headlights.

4. If you cannot drive because of thick fog stop the vehicle on extreme side of the road and keep the lights on.

Brake Failure

Do not panic if your brake pedal sinks to the floor

1. Pump the brake pedal several times fast and-hard, if this does not work.

2. Leave the accelerator and use hand brake and use slow and steady force.

3. Shift to lower gear.

4. Look for a place to stop.

5. Make sure your vehicle is off the road.

6. Switch on hazard lights.

7. Do not use the vehicle unless the defect is rectified.

Tyre Blow Out

With improved maintenance tire blow out is becoming rare as air leak is stopped and some air is left in the tires to prevent blow out.

1. Hold steering wheel tightly

2. Take your foot off the accelerator

3. Do not apply brake

4. Let the vehicle slow down to stop off the road

5. Apply brakes only when the vehicle is almost stopped

Steering Failure

It means vehicle will not turn when you turn the steering wheel

1. Take off your foot from the accelerator.

2. Let the vehicle slow down by itself.

3. Do not hit the brake until vehicle comes to a stop by itself.

4. In case of emergency of your vehicle hitting any other vehicle or person. Turn on emergency flashers and blow horn continuously to warn others.

Head Light Failure

1. Turn dimmer switch and then head light switch again. It may burn if there was loose contact.

2. If not put on parking lights.

3. Switch on hazard warning lights.

4. Pull off the road and leave hazard lights on.

5. Always carry spare fuses.

6. In case of blown out fuse replace with new one. It may restore the connection at least temporarily.

Struck Accelerator

1. Hook your toe under the accelerator pedal and try to lift it.

2. If it is not free, shift to neutral.

3. Brake vehicle to slow down.

4. Pull off the road as soon as you can.

Blocked Vision

If bonnet or hood suddenly open and block your vision

1. Roll down the window

2. Look around and have some view of the road

3. Look in rear view mirror for vehicles following you

4. Move to the edge of the road and stop

5. Turn on hazard warning lights

Vehicle Approaching You Head on in Your Lane

This is one of the life saving tips:

1. Slow down

2. Pull to your left, sound your horn

3. Do not pull to your right as the other driver may be pulling to his right and meet you head on

4. By moving away you can avoid head on collision

Vehicle Running Off the Pavement

The wheels may pull towards the left

1. Hold steering wheel tightly

2. Take your foot off the accelerator

3. Do not brake

4. When vehicle slows down gently correct the wheel back to the pavement

BE EXTRA CAREFUL BEFORE YOU CROSS
AN UNMANNED RAILWAY CROSSING

Stalling on Railway Track

Always take extreme care while crossing railway track manned or unmanned. If the train is approaching

1. Unfasten your seat belt ask all other passengers to do the same.

2. Ask them to get down and move away from the railway track and vehicle.

3. Run in the direction the train is coming from, there is a chance train may stop.

SAVE your life and those who are traveling with you. The driver's role starts only when he/she starts driving after getting the driving license.

Every moment of driving is important.

Buying a Vehicle

The most expensive fragrance in the world is the smell of a new car.

The decision to buy a vehicle is very personal, completely emotional and very often does not stand up to the scrutiny of cold logic and reasoning. The most expensive fragrance in the world is smell of the new car. Consumers are willing to spend thousands of rupees for that scent.

Remember you are the person who is going to drive, pay for the mortgage, maintenance and fuel bills. More than 85% of car buyers buy through financial companies.

Now-a-days buying a vehicle – either a car or a two-wheeler or any other vehicle for commercial or private purpose – are very easy. We have lots of options to choose from. Owning a vehicle is more of a necessity than luxury. Since the options are many, acquiring thorough knowledge about them is essential.

Buying a new vehicle is a choice for the purchaser. He/she should use extreme prudence before taking a proper decision.

Buyers are two categories.

First

Those who need a car:

Second

Those who want a car:

Factor for 'want a car' category, is size of packet (cheque book), check it and then go for it.

If you are 'need category,' sit and analyze your needs and also the Possible options.

a. Is there a reasonable and safe public transport – cost of such transportation – Annually add 25% for inflation and unforeseen travels.

b. Compare with cost of owning a car – include factors like

   i. Depreciation and resale value.

   ii. Cost of repayment for financial installment or loss of income from investment in case of outright purchase.

   iii. Cost of insurance.

   iv. Regular maintenance.

   v. Parking.

   vi. Inflation of all above costs.

   vii. Post and pre-warranty maintenance.

Other Options

a. Whether a small or big car.

b. Seat capacity.

c. Petrol or diesel. Or alternative fuels like LPG.

d. Availability of required fuel nearby.

e. How many different people are likely to drive.

f. Manual or Automatic gear.

g. Power or Manual steering or electronic.

h. Need of speed or economy.

i. Condition of roads.

j. Hatch back or sedan or SUV.

k. Nearest dealer and service station.

l. Other accessories like power windows, central locking, security systems etc.

m. Visibility or invisibility tinted windows.

Reduce choice to three or four cars.

Diesel engine cars are going to be better options. Tremendous improvement in diesel technology both in fuel as well as engine design and modern diesel engines have brought about admirable states like not rattling, shaking etc… They are now smoother and way ahead on fuel economy as well as longevity standards. Cost is high and may not be as responsive as petrol vehicles during driving.

When you want to buy a new vehicle.

i. Buy a vehicle you will own for a long time say 6–7 years.

ii. Buy what you want, and what you can afford.

iii. Do not think you have an upper hand in negotiations as dealers are seeing people like us every day. Their business is to sell, make profit for them and their company and in that order.

iv. Choose two or three vehicles and test-drive them before narrowing down your choices.

v. Confirm price, warranties, and other features, repairs, policy, defect proneness of the vehicle you want to purchase.

vi. Price of the car after all deductions and rebates.

vii. Interest rate, repayment terms, pre closing clauses, consult at least three or more auto financiers for the same type of vehicles before deciding.

viii. Always take a friend or neighbor who should be **programmed** to discourage you. This will help in negotiations.

ix. New car prices are highly competitive. More expenses are required to maintain a new car show room. You can time your purchase to get the best advantage.

Remember

Owing a car is much more than What it appears to be.

The moment you own a vehicle, Your responsibility starts.

Like electronic goods it loses its value as soon it leaves the show room.

In fact insurance value in 95% of the cost as soon as it leaves show-room.

Whatever be your mode of payment, you acquire a liability immediately.

No car has been designed so far, which costs zero maintenance and running.

All cars are provided with basic accessories., which are necessary for its basic functions. Add only accessories which are absolutely essential for your safety and comfort in that order, studies reveal that women are capable of choosing better options. Consult them before deciding.

You are responsible for pollution under control even to the vehicle, which is under warranty. Ensure you are very thorough with all provisions, which will lead to void of warranty and safe guard yourself. It may become a costly mistake.

Many factors like the duration you are going to keep the vehicle, initial cost, finance options, performance, warranty provisions, cost of running and maintenance are to be considered and weighed carefully. Then decide on new ear.

Pre-Owned Cars

If you are willing to do without fragrance of a new car, you can save thousands of rupees a year painlessly.

It is one of the best ways to set a head start in life. If you forego the prestige buying a new car, you can enjoy the prestige of being financially secured.

Buying a Pre-Owned (Used) Car

One of the advantages of buying a pre owned is a substantial cost saving of your money and liability. The negative aspect is it may lead to endless troubles and increased running and repair cost. Take extreme care before-buying.

In India we still have not developed a foolproof data collection system to have history of the car even you are ready to pay for the same.

Never indicate your eagerness in buying any particular used car. All pre owned car dealers offer different prices for the same year model cars because of its different usages.

What you do to evaluate the price of the old car, it is possible to get lost as a buyer, and the seller always make a tidy profit. Our efforts must be to reduce the tidy profit to the extent possible.

Tricks of finding a good pre-owned car

i. Unlike new cars, price is not the number. That is just a factor. Well-maintained and driven vehicles outweigh the price.

ii. Low mileage is not a good cause. In fact it is often a good reason for not buying as the speedo meter might have been tampered.

iii. Try to buy from reputed dealers of pre-owned cars, as almost all used car sellers are offering some kind of warranty.

iv. Do not field down to any particular model or dealer. Check from various sources.

v. In pre-owned cars with same model and similar mileage condition of the vehicle will vary.

vi. Find a price, which is too good to be true as you may be quite lucky in getting the real value for your money.

vii. Never hurry the salesman. Let him take his own time. Use ads in various papers and magazines to learn about the price range.

viii.   Once you decide tell the seller your conditions and if he is not meeting your deadline call it off.

Checking an Used Car

a.   Sight along both sides of car, misaligned panels, and difference in paint, shade indicate accidents check this in clear daylight.

b.   Check for rust by using a small magnet, near door panels, bottom floorboards, and mudguards and near dicky. All are made of magnetic iron. If magnet does not stick, it means major collusion damage and hence avoid buying.

c.   Stains on upholstery, on floor mats means rain leaks.

d.   Check for any leaks. Test drive vehicle for about 10 kilometers. Bring back to the same place and leave it for 10–15 minutes any leaks will normally show up.

e.   On a quiet road, run and apply brakes suddenly. If vehicle is pulling to one side it means uneven braking.

f.   On a level road, drive straight and leave the steering. The car should not pull to one side. It means accidents or misalignment.

g.   Try all controls and accessories for proper working.

h.   Switch on ignition and check all warning lights.

i.   Check for clutch. Depress the clutch, engage first gear. Repeat this in succession for a few times. Defect in clutch will result in crash during engagement.

Be watchful when buying old vehicle

Accelerate in low gear up to 20 Kmph. Release accelerator. Allow engine speed to drop and suddenly accelerate to full. See for blue or black smoke. If the smoke is blue or black, it shows excessive oil consumption or incomplete combustion.

Whether you buy a new or pre-owned vehicle ensure the vehicle makes you comfortable and confident. It should also add to your safety by giving you greater control.

The only way to determine how comfortable you are with a vehicle is to try it out as you get in or out of the vehicle, notice whether you have to bend awkwardly or have difficulty in maneuvering to come out or get in... This is not only for you, but also for other people who are likely to drive the vehicle. Check for blind spots caused by vehicle design, and whether you can adjust the mirrors for visibility on all sides?

Also ensure you can operate all the controls and pedals easily. All these are important in selecting a vehicle. You may like to spend more amounts if necessary to have the desired model.

Once you decide to buy insist on the following:

a. Vehicle registration certificate in original. Get it verified from Transport authorities independently. The expenses are worth the effort.

b. Insurance policies in original and valid.

c. Pollution under control valid certificate.

d. If the car from any other state get No Objection Certificate from concerned RTO. Do not buy even in case of smallest doubt; it may be a stolen vehicle.

e. Record date, time and place of sale. They are important to safeguard you from any legal consequences of possible misuse.

f. Transfer Ownership and insurance in your name immediately.

Selling your old vehicle

Do not forget your responsibilities while selling your old vehicle.

1. Give your vehicle a well-maintained look.

2. Pay attention to engine and battery cleanliness is most Important.

3. Take care of exterior and interior.

4. Take a good shine of painting.

5. Attend to minor repairs like lights, horn, wipers etc.

6. Tires keep them clean and properly inflated.

7. Get pollution certificate.

8. Never handover the keys in a hurry. Take at least two or three of your friends while the buyer test the vehicle.

9. Deliver only after receiving full payment. In case of cheque payments, do not handover the documents until the cheque is realized.

10. Keep the record of sale, mention the new owner's name, full address, phone no. Driving license no. etc. The list is just illustrative and not exhaustive, If necessary ask for proof of residence. Specify the date, time & place

of sale; get the buyer's signature and sign it yourself. Keep a copy with you.

11. Immediately inform RTO of the area where the car was registered enclosing a Xerox of the sale deed.

12. Inform your insurance company about the change in Ownership.

Today the average dealer makes more money in profit in used car sales than new cars. Some of the pre-owned cars are as good as new ones. So a new word 'Newsed car[1] has of late been coined to indicate new used cars.

Having purchased a used car you must also know to maintain and use it economically. Now a day's lots of low cost new cars are available.

Normal life of a well-maintained car is over 200,000 kilometers on average. So economics of major repairs like engine, transmission systems should be worked out. After repairs the vehicle should give at least 50000. kilometers. If not it is not worth the repairs, and you may consider giving it away and go for new one. Future repair costs are going to be prohibitively high.

Last, but not the least after you bought your vehicle new or used do not believe anything you hear from friends and family members. They did not buy cheaply. Car buying stories should be trusted as much as fishing stories. Might be they wanted to hide certain aspects in which they could have been duped. After all nobody wants to advertise their foolishness.

Having purchased a new or pre-owned vehicle you must calculate the annual cost of owning.

A. Ownership Cost

1. Payment depreciation example

    Cost 3 lacs

    Model value after 5 years Rs. 1.25–1.5 Lac

    Yearly depreciation Rs. 30000

2. Finance payment or interest lost

3. Insurance

4. Registration and License

5. Pollution and fitness

6. Road taxes (Annual or life time/years)

7. Cost of minor and major repairs

    Total = A

B. Annual Operating Cost

Average consumption; calculate total fuel bills plus cost of coolants, oils, repairs, tires and batteries.

Total = B

C. Parking Charges

Tolls.

Total = C

Total-operating cost = A + B + C, divide this amount by total kilometers run by the vehicle and it will give you Cost per kilometer per year.

It may vary and it will increase with age of the car.

Whether you have purchased a new or pre-owned car take care of the vehicle and become an exemplary driver/owner.

* * * * *

Used car dealer to customer:

This car has very low mileage. The former owner only drove it when he could get it started.

Nothing gives used car more kilometers per liter than the sales man.

Insurance

Insurance originated from the concept of unavoidability of accidents completely. In the event of any accident whether minor or major, it is necessary to safe guard the interests of all concerned.

It will be preferable and realistic to start this chapter with a real life incident. The sequence of the event runs as follows.

Name of the deceased	:	Ragesh kumar Goel
Job	:	Business of Paper and Export
Event	:	Night of August 28, 2000

He was driving his car in national highway I, in non-lit portion of Delhi-Karnal Sector. His vehicle hit a Tata Sumo Parked in Central verge of highway without any indication of burning hazard Warning lights. Mr. Goel died on the spot because of the accident. The insurance Co., was Oriental Insurance Co., New Delhi.

Case tried by Motor Vehicles Accident Tribunal Delhi by the Tribunal Judge. Mr. Girish Kath Palia. His (Goel's) Annual Income was about Rs. 2 Crores a year and he was spending Rs. 1.41 Crore a year for family. Judge remarked 'The compensation must be neither a pittance nor a bonanza.' He awarded compensation of 14.17 Crores to the next of kin on April 2005. One of highest ever compensations awarded in a Motor vehicles Accident Case.

The above incident is narrated so that the readers know, that adequate compensation can be paid to the aggrieved family but it can be a long drawn process. Imagine the hardship and pain the family has to undergo.

It also gives the imperative necessity of automobile lighting.

Every motor vehicle should be designed and maintained, so that it remains under absolute control of the person driving the vehicle at all times. Most of the drivers are well aware of the safety in driving and do their best to avoid any accident by using their sound and prudent judgment.

No sane person wants an accident Accidents do not happen, they are caused due to some underlying flaw or error of one or more persons. It causes bodily injuries, multiple fractures, deaths and loss of properties. It increases the work of medical professionals, traffic police, courts, etc. All of them are avoidable.

Lots of measures are being taken by various agencies connected with transport and road safety. Many hospitals, highway patrols have established trauma care and accident care units to cater for emergencies. Police and ambulance services are available 24 × 7, to cater for emergencies. The first hour known as golden hour immediately after the accident is vital and very useful for life saving. Proper treatment given to the injured during this time can save lives and reduce impact of injuries considerably.

Insurance originated from the concept of unavoidability of accidents-completely. In the event of any accident, it is necessary to safeguard the interests of all concerned, whether they receive minor or major injuries. The damage to the vehicles and properties are to be safeguarded.

The purpose of insurance is precisely the same. We need insurance at all times. We have a choice about our own life and properties, but for your vehicles you need it legally. It is illegal and a punishable offence to drive a vehicle without proper insurance.

There are two types of insurance policies. Package (comprehensive) and liability (Third Party) liability policy is compulsory and package policy is optional.

- Third party bodily injury or property damages liability for bodily harm or death is unlimited to the amount as awarded by the judge.

- Liability to property is limited to 7.5 lac rupee for four-wheeler.

- Personal accident cover up to Rs. 2 lac on death risk for the owner or driver.

- Besides this third party policy also provides cover for employees of owner of the vehicle injured or killed while traveling or using a vehicle as permissible under workmen compensation Act.

Package or Comprehensive Insurance

This covers all the liability insurance coverage and also damages caused by accidents and other unfortunate incidents. In the unfortunate event that the car is a total loss, the insurance company is liable to pay you the car's insured declared value (IDV) at the time of loss.

The IDV for new vehicles is taken as 95% of ex-showroom price. The value depreciates by 5% within six months, going up to 50% for cars aged four years or more the liability package may be cheaper. Complete package with different coverage's will be costlier but it will be a good idea to go in package policy if you are going to drive the car daily and use it extensively.

All cars purchased through finance companies will have to be comprehensively insured.

The package insurance covers

1. Accidents

2. Fire, explosion, self-ignition and lighting

3. Riots and strikes

4. Earth quakes

5. Floods, typhoon, hurricane, storm, cyclones and hopefully Tsunami

6. Burglary, house braking and theft

7. Malicious acts

8. Terrorism

9. Inland transit by road rail or waterways

Premium payable for a motor vehicle is based on

a. The motorist's age and of people likely to travel in the vehicles

b. Driving record

c. Job/Occupation

d. Country of Origin

e. Use of vehicle for business or pleasure

f. Place of garage

g. Make and model and year

h. Its value

Best Terms	Worst Term
Accountants	Professional
Bank Officials	Sportsmen
Civil Servants	Entertainers
Barristers	Night Club workers
Fire Brigade People	Hawkers
Opticians	Scarp Metal Merchants
Policemen	Foreign Service Person
Clerics	
Teachers	

As per the study carried out extensively most accident-prone drivers are aged 18 to 20 and 70 to 80 years. Safe drivers are between 50 to 60 years.

Always drive carefully. Safe driving is sane driving and avoids any type of accident and save you of all problems.

In the event of any unfortunate accident occurring, even a small accident

1. Keep cool and concentrate on essentials.

2. Get help for any one who may be injured.

3. Call the police if the accident is serious.

4. Collect as much information about the accident as possible. Never omit any details even appearing to be minor.

5. Do not be side tracked about any argument of other people.

Never Admit Any Liability

6. Make a sketch of the spot indicating

   Width of the road.

   Main or secondary.

Whether the vehicle was on correct lane or side before the accident and at the moment of impact.

7. Whether proper signal was given like indicator or brake light etc.

8. If it is in night whether all mandatory lights were burning.

9. The date, time of exact location of the accident.

10. Name and addresses of all passengers, drivers of all the vehicles involved.

11. Nature and extent of injury.

12. Name of the other driver, license particulars if available, registration no, of the vehicles, damage to any other properties.

Every information gathered is important. In case the accident is minor and not involving any third party no police report may be required.

In case of any third party is involved or damage to property is involved first information report (FIR) is a must. This is a vital document for all future actions.

Inform your insurance company over phone, follow it by writing.

If vehicle is to be towed to some garage intimate the name of a garage and towing agency and the address. The cost is reimbursable to some extent. Some companies provide the service as part of their contract (like my TVS).

Keep copies of all letters, phone call details so that you know what you have committed. Never give wrong or unverified information.

Furnish all required information in the claim form.

The insurance company will detail surveyors for, on that spot and detailed survey and scrutinize the estimate given by the garage. These recommendations are very valuable for claim settlement.

You must have constant liaison with garage, surveyors, police and insurance company.

You must take personal interest and get approval for repairs from the insurance co., early.

Engage a consultant who knows both about the automobile and the insurance business as well.

Once the repairs are completed you must give a satisfactory repair report. It is better you take delivery of the vehicle; by paying the entire cost and get your money reimbursed by insurance company.

After all these exercises, you will find yourself poorer by a few thousand rupees as money reimbursed by insurance co., will be nowhere near the money spent by you.

There will be compulsory depreciation on metal parts, which may go up to 50% after 10 years. There are many more items like all plastic, fiber rubber items, which attract 50% depreciation as soon as vehicles start plying of the road.

Do not take any person's words for granted. Always insist on seeing and knowing the latest ruling and polices.

Study all details of your policy and know the exclusions and most important – never allow your policy to lapse. Always renew it in time. If you make payment by cheque ensure sufficient funds are available and cheques are not dishonored.

Two typical examples

If you have appointed a driver and the driver escapes with vehicle, it is not considered as theft, but breach of trust.

Another funny report about an accident, a customer in the report of an accident writes.

I was driving on the road carefully and suddenly a tree came in front of me.

Here it will be pertinent to mention about driving and employing a driver either part or full time.

As per the recent judgment of the Supreme Court, the owner of the vehicle is responsible to ensure that the driver who is appointed, to drive a vehicle is in possession of a valid driving license, for the type of vehicle he/she is authorized to drive. This rule applies to any body driving any vehicle. Non-possession of a valid license for the type of vehicle being driven, will absolve the insurance companies, of all liabilities arising out of any form of accident.

This is a very important legal matter that should be kept in mind. In addition it will always be of use to keep your self aware of such rulings, so that you are not caught in the wrong foot at any time.

How to get the most out of your vehicles insurance.

Drive carefully – no accident no claim is the best policy.

- **License:** Never drive or allow anybody to drive your vehicle when he/she is not in possession of a valid license for your type of vehicle. This is a serious matter and the insurance company is not liable for any eventuality.

- Fine print: Read fine print and in between lines look for any exclusion.

- No claim bonus: You can claim up to 50% of your premium as no claim bonus. Now most of the insurance companies are revising this policy, keep in touch with them for latest policy decision.

- In case of minor accidents not involving third party, weigh options of no-claim-bonus and cost of repairs. Remember once a claim is lodged your meter is brought to zero.

- Choices are plenty: Compare terms offered and benefits and choose the right policy.

- Premium Reducers: Like anti theft alarms, VIN etching parking in closed garages will give you premium reduction and avail them.

- Whenever you travel by road to Sri Lanka, Pakistan, Bangladesh etc. get temporary additional insurance cover for your own safety.

- Any modification, engine change, fitment of LPG, CNG system get them endorsed by RTO and inform the insurance company.

- Renew on time. Never allow the policy to lapse. It may cost you a fortune.

In Case If Your Vehicle Is Stolen

1. Lodge a police complaint immediately. This is extremely important to safeguard yourself in the event of your stolen vehicle being used for some unlawful activities. In case the registration and documents are stolen with the car immediately apply for duplicate copies.

2. Keep a close liaison with the police and know about the current position.

3. If the vehicle is not traced within reasonable period, get report from the police and inform insurance.

4. if you are lucky enough to get back your vehicle, inform all concerned.

(An interesting incident about this is narrated in 'real life incidents').

Having read all details you will always wish you would not be willing to undergo all turmoil. So, drive defensively and safely and DRIVE SAFE AND BE SAFE.

Last but not the least, insurance companies give some reduction in premiums if you have installed anti theft devices like vehicle identification number, burglar alarms etc. So make use of them. You are more than amply covered.

How Safe Is Your Car

Every 15 minutes a car is stolen. Every year vehicles worth Rs. 1000 crores are stolen. 40000 cars are being stolen in India every year. Only 10% of them are ever traced.

Three Modalities of Stealing

a. For fun joy rides, stolen for fun and later abandoned.

b. For criminal activities as a get away vehicle.

c. For profit by stripping down and sold as parts. Fetches 2–3 times of market value of the car.

If auto theft were a legitimate business it will rank as the 50th among fortune 500 companies.

Insurance reimburses only part of the value.

How to foil car thieves and car jackers?

1. Keep an eye on vehicles following you for any unusual behavior

2. Follow safest routes and rules as well

3. Do not pick up unknown persons, particularly in deserted places

4. Drive with your windows raised and doors locked

5. Drive in center lane so that you cannot be forced off the road

6. Keep the vehicle in good condition to avoid any breakdown

7. Keep car keys separately

8. Park in well lit, highly visible popular areas

9. At night select busy 24 hour attendants garages only

10. Carry all papers of the vehicle with you in person do not leave them in vehicle

11. Do not leave any valuables or articles in the vehicle where it can be seen from outside

12. If you are accosted outside your car hand over car keys and move away; your life is more precious than the car

13. Always look below and behind rear seats to ensure nobody is hiding in the car

14. If any armed thief demands you to open the car when the car is in red light, seek the police advice to high tail it out of them. Average human reaction time is between .5 to 1.5 seconds and in most cases that is enough time to get away

15. Use steering locks and etch your vehicle identification number on windshield and chassis

Some good news for future car owners in INDIA:

From April 1, 2007 maruthi udyog is introducing electronic immobilizer as a standard fitting. The immobilizer consists of three elements. It is provided with a unique identity molded ignition key. The key carries a secret code and communicates digitally with engine computer via a controller. The engine will start only when the secret code matches.

If a wrong key is inserted, it will immobilize the computer and engine will not start. The device is expected to drastically reduce the car thefts to a great extent. As the theft risk is reduced the insurance premium will also likely to be reduced in future.

This will be a real silver lining for the future motorists. This is one avenue where technological development will directly bring benefit to the end user (the owner of vehicle).

Ensure your vehicle is insured against all possible risks and the policy remains valid at all times. In the insurance policy you will find the following wordings' policy will be in force till midnight of the 1ast day of validity." It literally means, if you do not renew your policy before the due date, the policy will stand lapsed from 0.01 hours following the midnight. If any unfortunate accident occurs before you renew the policy you are not entitled to get any compensation at all.

In India since 2000 Road Length has increased by 39% But vehicles by 158%, 78% of Accidents caused by errant drivers due to over speeding and drunken driving.

Motor vehicle act had been amended in 2017 and 2018, to safe guard the interests of all forms to road users. It is a fact, that more than 6–7 crore vehicles are plying without any insurance. They should be traced and brought into insurance ambit.

Insurance companies can play major role in educating people their moral duty to avoid over speeding and drunken driving and reward them. They should play positive role as they will be direct beneficiary to the out come. They should settle all deserving cases for compensation and this will be their best contribution to society.

So insure and be secure, and never allow your policy to lapse.

* * * * *

Amusing Court Award

19 Year old CARL Trueman of Los Angles won $ 74000 (Rs. 2.8 Lacs) when his neighbor ran over his hand with a Honda accord, Trueman apparently did not notice there was some

one at the wheel of the car, when he was trying to steal his neighbor's hub cap

* * * * *

Policemen to Motorist: You are driving at 65 Kmph against speed limit of 50 Kmph.

Motorist: No I am driving at 50 Kmph only.

They started Arguing.

Motorist's wife intervened and told the policemen not to argue with her husband when he is drunk.

Roads

Today INDIA can boast of having the highest motor able road and bridge built by Border roads organization. At highest point it climbs 18640 feet above sea level. It is KHARDUNLA PASS, in KASHMIR. This is held in GUINNES BOOK OF WORLD RECORDS.

Various forms of roads existed all over the world, which were used by men. Initially it was a footpath. Later on when men started domesticating animals, bridle paths were formed for transporting men and materials. Men used such roads, which existed 15000 years ago.

With invention of wheels, requirement of roads had changed drastically. In India we find references of roads since Ramayana and Mahabharata periods. They were used for plying of chariots. In Greek and Roman periods wheeled vehicles were used for trade and military purposes.

In India Roads were existing in 3500 BC which were found out during the excavations of Mohanchadoro – Harappa civilization sites. They were mainly used for administration and military purpose. During 500 BC Kautilya (chanakya) the chief minister of Chandra Gupta Maurya had laid down in Artha Sastra, the specifications for roads, and even recommended punishments for obstructing traffic.

Later years emperor Ashoka had constructed roads, which were mainly used for movement of Army and trade.

During the Mughal period Mohamed Bin Tuglak built road from Delhi to Daulatabad. Sher-sa-Suri built Delhi-Agra Road, which is still considered to be one of the best-aligned roads.

During British rule, Lord Dulhousie, Viceroy took keen interest in developing Grand Trunk Road and an important place Mughal Sarai (The road of the Mughal) is an important landmark.

During 1928, Indian Government had appointed Mr. A.R. Jayakar to go into the various aspects of road construction. The recommendations are more or less forms the present day rules.

Since the invention of wheels, roads are playing an important role in Transportation. Road is basically defined as 'an open way for vehicles, person, animals especially one lying out side of an urban limit.'

From olden times till today the basic aim of road construction is to facilitate comfortable movement of men and materials.

Present day requirement of roads demand a lot of skill and engineering Acumen. In fact construction of roads is one of the major industries and requires millions of rupees investment.

In India during 2005 we had

65569 Kilometers	National Highways
131899 Kilometers	State Highways
467763 Kilometers	District Roads
2650000 Kilometers	Rural and other Roads

Total of 33 Lakhs Kilometers Roads.

As the name itself implies the standards of roads are different. Similar with most of the countries National Highways form only 2% of the total roads but handle more than 40% of the traffic. They also account for major portion of road related accidents and economic loss. Majority of the trucks and buses ply on National Highways at an average of 3.3 Million kilometers every day.

Government of India, had launched the most ambitious golden quadrangle road project connecting Delhi, Mumbai, Chennai and Kolkata and other important feeder roads to cater for the country's future traffic needs. The total length of the golden quadrangle is more than 6500 kilometers. 70% of the goods is transported by road and we are adding kilometers daily.

The main purpose of this chapter is give an over view of various aspects involved in road construction, so that we know how important it is to maintain the road.

Construction of roads is one of the major industries and requires lot of efforts. It is a most demanding work. India like other developed countries had achieved total equipment oriented road construction technology.

It will be worth knowing various aspects of road construction so that all understand its importance as every one of us is a road user.

First

The mandatory locations and likely routes connecting them are decided... Aerial survey and physical walking on the tracks are done before finalizing the alignment. This is known as recee.

Second

Depending on the economic feasibility and likely density of traffic, based on populations the type of road and its structure are determined and the cost of construction may vary from a few laths rupees per kilometer to 3 to 4 crores per kilometer depending on the classification and design.

Various activities in road construction are:

a) Earth work

This means selection of basic road surface and fill it with approved quality of soil and compact it to the recommended degree. This basically forms the load-carrying element of the road.

b) Sub Grade

Once earth work is compacted, the surface must be filled with boulders/stones of approved size and quality and compacted.

c) Wet mix Macadam

Once the sub grade is completed in all respect, it is followed by laying a mixture of gravel, stone dust and accepted percentage of water and rolling it to required degree of compaction. Proper compaction at every stage is of utmost importance.

d) Binder Course

After the wet mix macadam, the road is completely dried and made dust free. It is treated with mild cure (mc'0") and Rapid cure (Rc2) bituminous mixture. This will form bonding surface for asphalt laying. This is a course mixture with less bitumen and other approved percentage of aggregates.

This and the next two activities require asphalt mixing plants, pavers and rollers.

The mixture should be laid at correct temperature and compacted.

e) Wearing Courses

This is the final layer of bitumen and aggregate, which is laid and rolled.

f) Seal Coat

This is a mixture of bitumen and extremely fine stone dust. This forms a sealing coat. It gives an aesthetic and clean image to the road.

Bridges

These form part of the road construction as the roads will have to pass through many water ways, chasms, gorges in mountain, back waters and rivers. Building bridges are more complicated in design and execution. It requires highly specialized skills, equipment and machineries.

In India, Ministry of Surface Transport (MOST) gives the specifications for all road construction activities. This corresponds to international specification for road construction. the roads are brought to finished state, necessary marking centerlines, berms, road signs, milestones are installed.

Various tests are carried out at different stages by extremely competent consultants. They ensure total quality control.

Last, but not the least, to maintain the roads, in the same condition and to restore them to original condition, periodical maintenance and repairs are absolutely essential.

Water stagnation is number one enemy for the roads. Famous civil engineers' quote on proper construction and maintenance is 'most important' aspect of road construction and maintenance are Drains, Drains and Drains.'

Some of the major reasons for the present awful condition of majority of our roads are

a. Failure to provide necessary drains, neglecting the cardinal principle of road building.

b. Use of substandard materials and methods.

c. Lack of awareness and understanding between various agencies and public.

d. Legal loopholes in taking action against violation. According to the survey carried out by NDTV during November 2005, Banarghetta Road in Bangalore was awarded 'The Worst Road in India.' This should be an eye opener for all.

e. Misuse of roads by unscrupulous elements by heavy overloading and over speeding, rash and negligent driving. A broken down vehicle with a burst tire, running on an asphalted road can damage the road considerably by gouging out the road surface. This will be very difficult to repair.

Border Roads Organization (BRO)

It will be worth mentioning about the above organization here with its Head Quarters in New Delhi. It had achieved extraordinary level in construction of roads and bridges in Trans Himalayan region from the plains of Rajasthan to the wild forests of Mizoram, Tripura.

Thousands of engineers and workers, braved most hostile weather of below freezing temperatures, very heavy rainfall regions and arid deserts.

Scores of men sacrificed their lives, during construction. Today India can boast of highest motor able road and bridge built at the highest altitude in the world. This is KHARDUNGLA PASS in KASHMIR. At the highest point it climbs 5682 Meter (18640 feet). Constructed by BRO in 1976 and opened for motor vehicle in 1988. This is held in GUINNESS BOOK OF WORLD RECORDS.

Started in May 1960, BRO is having 35000 regular employees and over 70000 casual laborers and had constructed more than 34000 kilometers of road in the most inhospitable regions and regions once thought to be unreachable. It had brought development to most of the Border States in the north, east and northeast regions.

The organization is growing and ready to meet any challenges in road construction. BRO had constructed roads in Bhutan, Mayanmar, Bangladesh, and Afghanistan. In cases of wars, natural calamities etc restoration of communication was achieved in shortest possible time because of exemplary work of BRO personnel. They are trained and have the mind set to achieve the impossible with ease. This is the only organization in the world to achieve such landmarks. We may or may not travel in their roads but we owe them our highest regards for their service. The author had the privilege and honor of serving in the organization for more than 28 years and is extremely proud of it.

This information is given so that everyone understands the importance of road construction and necessity to maintain the roads. It is by no means an encyclopedia of road building.

The floods occurred in Tamilnadu and Mumbai is 2005 due to unprecedented rains showed the importance of drains. There was water logging all over, because of lack off proper drains.

The rain during October November was the heaviest in the last 100 years. Proper drains could have solved majority of the problems.

While reading about roads it will be interesting to know about China's roads. It is on its highway to prosperity at a fantastic rate.

Chinese **national expressway network** is the apex agency.

In 1998 china did not have a single kilometer of high way conforming to international standards.

In 2006 it has 41000 Km of highways (next only to USA).

Till 1990 India was way ahead of China in road construction.

From 2001 to 2006 China built 24000 Km of express highways 4800 Km in a year – 14 Km per day, unparalleled in history.

Their road network is 7-9-18. 7 from capital Beijing and 9 from north south and 18 from east west.

In 1990s a journey of 100 kilometers used to take one day.

Now it takes about 1 or 2 hours only.

The highways are literally china's roads to the 21st century.

ROADS FOR THE FUTURE; In future proper construction and maintenance of roads are going to play an all – important role. A well-maintained road will reduce the risk of road related accidents considerably. It will also reduce the congestion by reducing the time of travel and increase comfort while driving.

It is estimated that in MARYLAND USA, more than 3 billion dollars are lost due to congestion in roads. This is in addition to loss due to accidents. All are avoidable losses. A well-maintained road and regulated traffic, safe, sensible, drivers and well maintained vehicles could cumulatively save crores of rupees of avoidable loss to the nation.

To end this with a positive note, the best vehicle and road combination as described in a novel is given.

In Germany, a Jaguar car was planted with a bomb, which was set to explode, when the front suspension springs are closed and the coils are in complete contact. The driver being unaware of the bomb drives the car for more than 1000 Km. The vehicle was driven in autobahns in Germany and explosion never takes place.

The reasons are superior construction of autobahns and excellent functioning of the suspension system of the Jaguar Car during the entire Journey.

Road Users

All of us are road users in one form or other. Most of the problems in road related accidents are due to improper use.

The road users can be classified into two categories

Normal Users

1. Pedestrians
2. Cyclists
3. Two wheeler riders
4. Autos
5. Cycle Rickshaws
6. Cars/Buses/Truck
7. Bullock Carts
8. Hand Carts
9. Specialist Vehicles
10. Any other mode of approved transport

Misuse/Abuse

1. Owner of roaming cattle
2. Children and adults using road as play ground
3. Kite flying on road

4. As night shelter

5. Road side workshops

6. Storage place for goods

7. Begging or hawking

8. Wrong parking place

9. Other professional activities

10. Unauthorized encroachment

11. Using roads and pavements for functions

Those who misuse the roads, are not only endangering themselves, but also cause inconvenience to other normal road users. They are directly and indirectly responsible for many accidents. Those persons sleeping on pavement lost their lives, because they used it as night shelter.

In India the social conditions force millions of people to use pavements and roads as night shelter.

Particularly errant drivers expose them to road related accidents.

Unfortunately we always tend to ignore commonest things and even worse we become unfortunate victims for no fault of ours.

What can we do?

As drivers of various forms of transport., while driving, particularly in night or during inclement weather like rain, fog etc, take care to look for people using pavements as dwelling places. Also Children might be playing unconsciously around without realizing the risks.

As one of the road users, make sure you are safe guarding your self against accidents. Ensure your children do not wander. Keep them under your care all the time.

As far as possible do not misuse the road, discourage begging and hawking, more so particularly at the Road junctions and around the signal points. I have observed locations at the road signals to be resourcefully converted as begging places. Mostly perhaps the rich car users dole them out some small coins. HOW I WISH I HAD THE POWER TO ADVISE THEM NOT TO DO IT ANY MORE. If only the beggars are not allowed to do begging at such points, one important source of accidents can be stopped.

Be considerate to elderly persons and help them. Learning elements of safety is not difficult, for which no formal education is required, and practically at no cost. All of us are endowed with abundant common sense and we should use it all the time. That is the only and main requirement.

It is possible and also our basic duty and responsibility to be a safe road user. Keep children well within your control while they accompany you walking on the road.

Let us thrive to be exemplary road users and set example to others to follow.

Cyclists and Two Wheeler Riders

The riders of two wheelers are very much vulnerable to accidents, because they are totally unprotected.

The cyclists and two wheeler riders form part of the majority of road users. The numbers of cycles, motorcycles and mopeds scooters are on the increase. Almost 15000 vehicles are added every day on the roads. Slowly motorcycles and scooters are replacing most of the bicycles. Total population of two wheelers form 70% of total vehicles in the country. Tamilnadu has the maximum number of two wheelers in the country, and also heads the fatality list of deaths due to road accidents. This is because cars are still a luxury for most of us and train and bus travels are cumbersome and two wheelers offer greater mobility and independence. The riders of two wheelers are very much vulnerable to accidents because they are totally unprotected.

The chances of fatality are 14 times as great for two wheelers as for car drivers. But unhappy feature in a cycle is a large number of accidents are associated with it. It is because it offers no protection to the rider in the event of a collision.

The types of accidents are collision-and fall. Main causes are

➢ Making improper turns or rather unwise decisions to turn.

➢ Disregarding traffic signals and signs.

> ➤ Double or triple riding.

> ➤ Improper maintenance of roads – potholes.

Three important aspects are important and must be cultivated by any driver – cyclist, two-wheeler driver, car driver or a lorry driven. They are

1. Rich common sense

2. Faultless anticipations

3. Unfailing judgment

By providing separate cycle tracks and enforcing them by law will reduce the accidents to almost zero.

If you are a cyclist; you must-

a. Never travel more than two abreast.

b. Do not use foot ways.

c. Use only cycle tracks where provided or use extreme left side of the road.

d. Do not hang on to any fast moving vehicles.

e. Avoid double and triple riding. Particularly on imbalanced roads.

f. Provide your cycles with good brakes, night reflectors and lamps.

In-foreign countries wearing a crash helmet is compulsory for all cycle riders.

Another main cause of concern is that two wheeler drivers are victims and generally succumb to head injuries. This points to usefulness and absolute need for wearing crash helmets. The very word indicates it is the helmet, which will crash if at all, and not your head.

Always protect your soft ware (Brain) by wearing the hardware (helmet).

If you are a two-wheel rider in the interest of your own safety and safety of your pillion riders you must.

a. Never drive even for short distance without wearing crash helmet.

b. Compulsorily provide rear view mirror on both sides.

c. Compulsorily provide screen or sari guards to the rear wheel so that loose garments do not get entangled in the spokes of rear wheels.

d. Restrict the number of riders to the driver, and one pillion rider only. Both must wear crash helmets.

e. Do not carry any pillion rider when you have only a learner's license.

f. Compulsorily provide footrest for pillion rider.

g. Follow the speed limits and not weave through the road.

h. Reduce vehicle speed to suit road conditions like rain, oily surface, or bad roads, as two wheelers are more susceptible to skidding.

i. Maintain your vehicle in good shape; brake lights must be in order so that the other road users can see them clearly during night and rainy season.

j. Do not drive or allow others to drive without proper valid license.

k. Never drive vehicle without proper insurance coverage and relevant papers.

l. Last, but not the least, never – drive under influence of liquor or any form of drug.

Most of us might buy a new motorcycle or scooter. You must know how to use a new vehicle. First, you must read the owner's manual of the vehicle very thoroughly and must often revise it in keep you updated.

Few tips are given which are general to all two wheelers

1. The first 500–600 Km is the crucial part of life of any new vehicle proper running in by following the guide-lines or speed limits, not exposing engine to excessive heat and driving with special care and restraint are important.

2. Proper running in driven vehicle the reliability and performance will increase.

3. Know all the controls and parts of the vehicle. They are clearly marked in the manual.

4. Inspection before riding

    a. Engine oil – Availability to the level.

    b. Fuel: you must have enough fuel as per your plan for use.

    c. Tires.

    i. Check pressure

    ii. Adequate tread depth

    iii. No cracks on or oil deposits sticking to the tires

  d. Battery: Proper working of horn, lights, and electrolyte level.

  e. Head lights, low and high beam, speedometer, lamp etc.

  f. Steering, smoothness no play or looseness.

  g. Throttle: Correct play in cable smoothness.

  h. Brakes effectiveness and correct play.

5. As far as possible initial starting in mornings should be by kick-start.

6. Stopping and parking

  a. Close the throttle completely

  b. Apply both brakes simultaneously

  c. Turn the ignition off

  d. Park the vehicle on a firm flat surface

  e. Lock and remove the ignition key

7. Applying both brakes gently will improve braking effort and reduce stopping distance.

8. On a wet, sandy or uneven surfaces or while taking turn application of brakes may result in skidding and loss of control. Ride slowly and safely.

9. Park vehicle in shade.

10. Drive at 40–45 Km/Hour (Economy mode). This is safe and fuel-efficient way to drive.

11. Avoid frequent braking and also anticipate stops.

12. Wear proper riding apparel and do not wear loose garments; they are unsafe.

13. Do not try to show your skills on road.

14. Proper posture

    a. Elbows are held inside close to the body,

    b. Hold both arms at an angle of 120°.

    c. Hips should be in a position which is comfortable to you.

Ensure that arms and shoulders are relaxed.

    d. Do not gaze at one point.

    e. Relax to guard against sudden impact.

    f. Point the toes straight ahead.

    g. Do not use cell phones while driving.

    h. While cornering reduce speed and be stable.

15. While braking hold the vehicle in upright position. Be a safe driver for your own sake and for the sake of other road users.

This chapter will not be complete without a special mention about the menace caused by majority of people without realizing the consequences they are:

a. Braking of pumpkins on new moon days to ward off evils and bring in prosperity. This is a major event in many parts particularly southern India. A broken pumpkin on the road acts as icy surface, over which two wheelers will skid easily. The rider will lose the balance and crash. The injury will be directly proportional to the speed.

b. Similarly breaking of cocoanuts on roads. The fragment of coconut shell can easily puncture the tire and cause skidding. Police authorities always request the public not to do such things on roads by announcements in TV, Radio, and newspapers regularly. The menace is on reduction mode. But it can be totally prevented by cooperation of all.

For their own safety two wheeler riders are advised to refer to almanacs to know in advance and drive with extreme care to avoid any untoward incident.

Selection of Helmets

Helmets are lifesavers for all two wheeler drivers and pillion riders. This has been proved beyond any doubt. Therefore selection of proper helmets is very important. The helmet should give you safety and comfort in that order.

When you select a helmet do not hurry. Spend at least 15 to 50 minutes before finalizing. Wear the helmet with all locks and straps. You should be comfortable in the helmet. If it is too tight it will not be comfortable, If it is loose it will become dangerous in case of an injury, as a loose helmet will cause more damage.

The straps holding your lower jaws should be comfortable to wear and allow movement of your lower law allowing you to speak it should be touching your ear lobes, but not pressurize the ear lobes to cause pain.

The neck support must be gentle. Initially some pain may be felt. Once you wear it for sometime, it will become less and you will feel comfortable. If the pain in your neck persists it will not be good for you.

When purchasing the helmet, extract an assurance in writing that it is original and confirm to ISI standard. Also after wearing it for sometime, if you feel uncomfortable, you can exchange it for a suitable one.

Repairing a damaged helmet and selling it, as a new one is the most dangerous sale. It is worst than a spurious spare.

Never buy from an unauthorized, unknown, source. Insist on a bill of sale and preserve it.

To check whether ISI stamping is genuine or not we can refer website www.bis.org.in or in Chennai you can ring up 044-22541442 or 22541216 the serial no of the ISI sanction will be on the top and manufacturer's name will be in the bottom.

Motorist complains to Policeman when so many people are violating traffic, why do you catch only me?

Policeman: when I go for fishing, I am not catching all the fish in the river.

* * * * *

Policeman to Scooter Driver: Why you are driving without light in the night?

Scooter driver: Today is full moon day. There is plenty of moonlight. I do not need any light in my scooter.

Policeman: OK. After deflating both tires says there is air all around the world. So you do not need any air in your scooter tire drive on.

* * * * *

A smart guy wanted to demonstrate his riding skill of motorbike.

He was riding with both feet off sayings 'now I am riding without my feet.'

Next he announced 'now I am riding without my hands, with both hands off the bike.'

Next as expected he crashed along with his bike. Now he shamefully admits 'now I have no teeth.'

(Moral of the joke – never try to show your riding skills on roads. Keep them for circus).

* * * * *

Pedestrians

Pedestrians are the largest individual road users and also form a large percentage in road related accidents.

Pedestrians: persons other than drivers or passengers. Persons in or operating a pedestrian conveyance such as perambulator, invalid chair without engine, push cart or pulling a cycle are pedestrians. Persons attending to a vehicle (example for changing a tire or repairing engine etc), moving on roller skates are also pedestrians.

They are subjected to maximum risks as road users.

Senior Citizens as Pedestrians

Remember, senior citizens are likely to be victims of pedestrian accidents because of their impaired vision, reduced hearing and slow in reaction.

They should

a. While crossing the roads make allowances for their age related problems.

b. Never try to cross the roads in unauthorized crossings, but only on marked or zebra crossings along with others never try solo (alone).

c.   Wear light colored clothing or reflective strips. While walking on roads use pavements and in case pavement cannot be used, walk facing the traffic.

d.   While using umbrellas in rain or sun, take care to see both sides before crossing.

e.   Your safety must be your main concern. For other road users you are an impersonal object. They may or may not recognize your needs.

f.   If you are in the habit of taking medicines for any ailments like blood pressure, sugar, make sure you are perfectly all right before venturing out. **Other road users will not make allowances for your medical problems.**

g.   Cross the road briskly by shortest distance after ensuring the road is clear. Never hesitate to ask for help.

h.   Always use subways or pedestrian crossings where available.

i.   Beware of stepping behind a vehicle into the way of other vehicle

j.   Never mount or dismount from a moving vehicle.

k.   Always carry identification papers and important medical information about you. suffering from Diabetes, allergy to any particular drug etc. They will save lives in case of any unfortunate accident. Abroad, they have a pendant around the neck of a diabetic clearly carrying a badge indicating that the person is a diabetic. Diabetics are likely to suffer very low sugar or high sugar incidences unexpectedly.

LOOK BEFORE YOU CROSS,
AND CROSS ONLY ON ZEBRA CROSSINGS

Other Pedestrians

Remember all of us are in the process of becoming senior pedestrians whether we like it or not. It is an accurately timed process and sure to embrace every one of us.

So,

1. Always walk facing the on-coming traffic.

2. Cross the road in zebra crossings or controlled crossings.

3. Never jump or alight from a moving bus or vehicle.

4. Never try to cross in a crowded traffic by weaving.

5. Never assume your right of way, wear bright colored clothing, particularly while moving in rain. Use bright colored umbrellas so that drivers can identify you.

6. Help old and invalid people to cross the road by allowing unhindered movement.

Various Factors Influence Pedestrians

A) Time and its influence

i. Dark periods of heavy traffic usually cause frequent pedestrian accidents. This corresponds to rush hour traffic in the evenings.

ii. They are more during weekdays when traffic flow is very heavy.

B) Speed of walk

The average speed of walking is 0.75 to 1.8 meters per second. Normally it takes about 10 seconds to cross a road crossing.

In case of old, invalid people the speed is much less. Even though pedestrian crossings allow sufficient time for crossings children, fellow pedestrians must give old and invalid people more time.

A drunken pedestrian is more harmful than a drunken driver. He is a potential danger to fellow pedestrians, other road users and himself.

Women pedestrians are better than men and use intended crossings more frequently. They wait for more favorable gaps in vehicle stream when crossing, and then move.

C) Social condition

Probably due to lack of adequate training and education under privileged and low income people figure prominently in pedestrian calamities.

D) Driving Experience

Persons having driving experience are more careful as pedestrians. They understand fully the limitation of driver and other road users.

E) Road Lighting and Vehicle Lightings

Both lights are important so that both can see each other and better safety is achieved. This is particularly important during rain, fog and poor visibility.

Safety Measures: Duties of Authorities

1. Segregation of pedestrian crossings.

2. Provision of pavements for use of pedestrians.

3. Separate pedestrian phases where a heavy pedestrian traffic is involved.

4. Installation of Pedestrian actuated signals.

5. Provide sub ways or over bridges where traffic volume is very heavy.

6. Introduce one-way traffic wherever possible to facilitate safe movement of pedestrians.

7. Provide proper lightings at pedestrian crossings.

8. Provide guarded crossing near schools, hospitals and public places.

9. Ensure pavements are not misused.

10. Provide safety education to children and others regularly.

For all Pedestrians

Remember you have an obligation to live for your and your family's sake,

a. Walk defensively so that you are aware of the on coming traffic, the drivers can see you and you can see the driver.

b. Use subways, over bridges, zebra crossings, regulated crossings only.

c. Be patient before crossings. A few moments of delay can save your life. Better late than never.

d. Help elderly, disabled persons while crossing, since time is limited during crossing, render necessary assistance to authorities in maintaining the discipline in pedestrian crossings and roads.

e. Inculcate self-cultivated manners of road use. Teach your children, friends, relatives the importance of road manners.

f. Be aware that roads are meant for every body's use and never take other's consideration for granted. **You are the only person who can save yourself.**

g. Last, but not the least learn from women. They are better than men, be patient and use judgment.

h. Always carry your personal identification and important medical information.

Now the most important issue of all.

Remember, you are subjected to all risks whenever you use the road. So all precautions and safety measures are required to be followed at all times. There is no respite from this rule.

Most of the times pedestrians are involved in accidents due to no fault of theirs.

Sometimes the pedestrians misjudge the situation, or even plain stupidity might cause accident.

Whatever be the reason it is the pedestrians who either lose their lives or sustain serious injuries. In both cases, your family suffers.

Motor Vehicle Act had been amended in 2017 and 2018 to safe guard. Interests of all forms of road users. This is a boon for unfortunate pedestrians who fall victims of accidents.

This should be given wide publicity and good Samaritans must work for the poor and needy people.

Proper road traffic education to be given to all pedestrians so that we can prevent the incidents to great extent.

Legally all pedestrians are governed as third party in all automobile accidents. So they are entitled for compensation from insurance and motor vehicle accident tribunal.

Every one must know completely about their rights and entitlements.

* * * * *

One of my uncle was ran over by a road roller

Where is he now?

In hospital 1ˢᵗ floor from

Room No. 2 to 5.

* * * * *

My uncle was ran over when he was crossing the road when the light was red.

He should have waited for green light.

He could not because he was colorblind.

* * * * *

Children Future Citizens

Children laugh 115 times and ask 65 questions and engage in creative activities 98 times every day. They are basically inquisitive.

We all love our children and we want them to study well and get good employment and lead a comfortable life. It is our duty to do all we can, so that our children can face tomorrow's competitive world with confidence.

Today's children are going to be the future citizens and they are bound to enjoy the benefits of all developments. They also will have to face the consequences of man-made disasters and suffer the effects.

All children are born equal. They are basically inquisitive and do not have any sense of fear.

It is said the children laugh 115 times and ask 65 questions and engage in creative tasks 98 times in a day. Adults of age 40 laugh only 11 times and ask 2 questions and engage in creative tasks 6 times. Main reason is bringing up into much of controlled life. Children learn very fast and before 4 to 5 years they attain maximum learning capacity.

All people like parents, relatives, friends, teachers and others who are in constant contact with children will form ever lasting influence on them.

Children, who are brought in good environment, will automatically become good sensible citizens of future.

Future world is going to become more competitive and effects of developments are likely to be off set, because of explosive population growth.

Travel is going to be one of the major areas of development. Commuting 100 Km a day is going to be very normal.

Transport related benefits and problems are going to be core issues of future.

The very concept of road usage is going to change dramatically. Repairs of automobiles, maintenance will become fewer in frequency but going to cost very high.

Lots of built-in safety features will be included in the designs of automobiles, roads, and other infrastructures. But the ultimate responsibility to ensure safety will always rest on drivers and other road users only.

So the challenges for the next generation (children who are now 10 years or less) are going to be much more complex. There may not be an all round desirable development but problems of road users will increase considerably.

It will be a really tough task for future road users, as they will have the advantages of developments and disadvantages of immaturity of majority of road users.

The requirement of proper behavioral training in safe and sane road use cannot be overemphasized.

This is a collective task of parents, schoolteachers, license and traffic authorities, and medical professional people.

They should work together in tandem to achieve best results.

What parents can and should do:

a. Educate about road safety, more as a habit than discipline.

b. Let children realize, that they are forming safety habits for their own future benefits.

c. Take them to various seminars, exhibitions. Let them participate in safety campaigns along with other children.

d. When learning to drive, let them know proper use of the vehicle. Let them think of the vehicle as a living creature and respect their sentiments. Unfortunately there is no SPCA for vehicles.

In India, Road accident fatalities are no 2 in killer list. Most susceptible to fatalities are children of 5 to 18 years.

In 2010 road accidents fatalities will be no 1 in killer list.

India, which is having 1% of total vehicle population of the world, is responsible for 6% of road accidents fatalities. Main reasons are

a. Improper and inadequate medical facilities for treating victims of road accidents particularly in the first golden hour.

b. Lack of public awareness in taking any action in case of accidents, even telephoning to police/emergency (it is a toll free call) is not done.

c. Fear of law enforcement the informant will be asked to testify and even harassed and held responsible for accidents.

d. No strict action against traffic violation like drunken driving, over speeding, over loading and rash and negligent driving. And many more reasons.

Most of the cases children become causalities.

A child today is going to be a road user of tomorrow. Maybe as a driver, police, doctor, or a pedestrian or in any other form.

A well-trained child of today will become an asset. It is very much possible to train young minds. Once they realize, that all the training and advice are for their good and safety, it will be deeply embedded in their minds and will have an ever-lasting influence.

They will be displaying road mannerisms according to the type of road usage, which will compliment to each other. They will form a sensible and responsible society.

Another important issue, which the future generation of road users has to face, is 'how to reduce avoidable losses due to accidents and road congestion.' In INDIA we lose over 55000 crore rupees every year due to road related accidents. The loss due to congestion is yet to be estimated.

For example in MARYLAND USA. It is estimated that more than 3 billion dollars (1000 crore rupees) is lost due to congestion in roads every year. All are avoidable losses. It is the responsibility and moral duty of the young generation of today to find ways and means to reduce or eliminate the avoidable loss. A developing nation like INDIA, cannot afford to lose such huge sum.

All future citizens will be using one form of transport or other for commuting to their work place and back. For example husband and wife may be going to different places for work, at different timings. Their daily travel will cause lots of stress and strain to them due to various factors. Always give allowance for their emotions, and develop proper understanding.

As per the recent study such emotional stress is going to be one of the main causes for divorce and separation. This will be an additional, price they may have to pay for enjoying the benefits of development.

By becoming a safe and sane road user, they will find their own lives and lives of others., Completely different and enjoyable. Our own well being is a function of the well being of our fellow men.

* * * * *

Two green beans are crossing the free way when a truck hits one of them.

His friend scraps him and rushes him to the hospital. After hours of surgery doctor, says I have some good news and bad news.

Healthy bean asks what is the good news first?

Doctor say, well he is going to survive, but bad news in he will be a vegetable for rest of his life.

* * * * *

Future Cars

The increasing demand from customers and pressing problems on environmental pollution and gradual depletion of the fuel availability, pose several challenges for the future cars. It must satisfy all requirements and much more. It is a continuous virtuous cycle.

Every new automobile is more technically sophiscated than the model it replaces. Cars are already belonging to the most technically complex items owned by an average citizen, and every indication is that this trend will continue, In future cars, consumers will be ready to pay extra money for safety related devices like, Two stage smart air bags, run flat tires,. Active cornering headlights back up seats and blind spot detection etc, It is estimated buyers will be ready to pay even up to Rs. 1 lac or even more towards safety systems passenger protection and pedestrian safety. All future cars and vehicles will be loaded with lots of safety devices, and safety will be the foremost consideration.

The development of future cars is likely to be on the following lines.

a. Alternative fuels like LPG, CNG Ethanol, fuel cells and electric, solar powered cars.

b. More thrust will be given for prevention and reduce the probability of accidents and ensuring safety of all road users.

c. More electronic controls which are more sensitive in data collection and response to situations, enabling fastest data processing techniques for arriving at tangible decisions at quickest possible time.

Innovation percentage, which will have impact on future cars

1. Alternatively powered vehicles — 41%

2. Active collision avoidance systems — 27%

3. Wireless technology (blue tooth etc) — 14%

4. Advanced electrical and electronic controls — 9%

5. Passive injury mitigation – safety — 4%

Top Design and Engineering Challenges

Safety will be the top most aspect

1. Cost reduction   36%

2. Fuel economy   15%

3. Quality   6%

4. Others   29%

Growth of automobile industry in INDIA is phenomenal. Flexible fuel technology is very important to countries like INDIA, which abounds in many alternative energy sources.

We have abundant solar power available throughout the year. It can provide long-term cost effective solution.

India also can produce 300 billion liters of ethanol which is an alternative fuel to gasoline, we can save around

20000 crore rupees every year, if this alternative fuel in used. Now we are able to produce only 33 million tons as against our demand of 110 million tons.

Scope for using alternative fuels in India is unlimited.

From October 2007, as per Government of India's policy ethanol blended fuel must be used in all fuel filling stations. The ethanol content will be around 5 to 10%. This is going to some problems for non-ethanol compatible vehicles. Only 3–4 million vehicles out of 13 million vehicles are ethanol compatible. Running vehicles with 5–10% ethanol fuel is going to be very difficult for over 10 million vehicle owners. Tuning up the engine for ethanol compatibility is going to be a skilled job requiring special technicians and going to cost around 8000–10000 rupees.

It will be better for all future car buyers to ensure ethanol compatibility before buying new or pre owned vehicles.

Recently Defense Research and Development Organization (DRDO) had developed Jetropha based fuel as an alternative fuel to diesel and petrol. They were able to increase the extraction ratio from 30% to 35%. The likely cost will be around Rs. 30 per liter. They will be carrying extensive trial of the fuel in army tanks and other vehicles. Preset tests indicate no adverse effects on pollution and performance. It does not require any modification in engine design the residual waste obtained can be used as high protein animal feed.

Use of any alternative fuel will result in growing crops, which will produce the required alternative fuel either directly or as a by-product. In both cases lots of agricultural lands will have to converted into fuel based crops. This may not be a healthy development, for INDIA, which is basically an agricultural oriented country. The government should bear this in mind before proceeding in this direction.

Future Lightings

All future lights will be using xenon gases instead of conventional filaments. These lights are designed to last to the life of the vehicle and will run for approximately 2500 hours. They will provide almost 3 times the illumination of a halogen lamp. However for illuminating xenon lights we need 20000 volts corresponding to a spark plug in the gasoline engine. Once lit it will need only 12 volts to maintain the glow. Replacing lights will become a specialized job.

New Engine Technologies

The famous 1908 model T, Ford had a 2900 cc engine and developed 20-horse power. Still it was rated as one of the best engines of that era,

Today Ford fiesta engine of 1596cc develops around 101 hp, almost 5 times of the earlier T model. In addition the new engines are more reliable, quieter, fuel efficient and cause less pollution.

Nature has many wonders from where we can learn many things. The latest research in diesel fuel injection, the humble BEETLE teaches a brand new process. The beetle is only 2 centimeters in length,. It is capable of producing a hot spray of liquid at 100 degrees centigrade up to 16 centimeters (8 times of it's length). It is able to spray, 300 to 400 times in a minute, in the form of extremely fine particles, finer than spray used in – modern fuel injection systems. It does this in self defense.

Serious research is going on in a BRITISH university, how to duplicate this nature's wonder in diesel vehicle injection systems in future vehicles.

Engines are now so reliable and service intervals are so long that we forget that regardless of how good the engines are, lubricants and filters have to be routinely changed for optimum performance. Replacing lubricants and filters at recommended service intervals improves engine performance as well as delivers superior mileage.

Fuel cell powered vehicles: They are still in research and testing stage. We can catch up with the latest technology easily.

Electric Vehicles: Belgian Engineer Mr. 'Camille Jawatzy' developed first electric vehicle in 1899. It ran around 100 Km/hour start stop distance for 1 Km was 47.4 seconds.

An electric vehicle is a simple mechanical system consisting of a battery to supply energy. A drive motor to transmit it to the wheels and electronic control to regulate the whole system. It has a limited number of components which require no tuning and very little maintenance. consequently, electric cars offer very high operating reliability.

Electric Vehicles Offer:

a.   Increased driver's comfort and lower running cost.

b.   Noiseless in operation.

c.   Low vibration level.

d.   Fiber reinforced plastic body offers higher thermal insulation.

They have limitations

    a. End price is high.

    b. Replacement cost of batteries is also high.

    c. Limitation of maximum travel per charge.

Comparison of CNG and LPG

CNG	LPG
(Compressed Natural Gas)	(Liquefied Petroleum Gas)
Cost of conversion to double of LPG	Low cost of conversion
High compression ratio 14:5:1	Low compression ratio 10:5:1
Dead weight is more because of cylinder design	Less dead weight
Can be used for both petrol and diesel	More complicated modification required for diesel

Hydrogen Powered Engine

Liquid Hydrogen powered vehicle light duty car 'MUSASHI III' had already been tested in Japan at Maximum operated speed of 118 Km/hour. Still more research is going on

Some of the other developments

    a. The revolutionary reaction supplanting about 100 years of spring and shock absorber suspension system has been developed. The new concept has been developed by Mr. Amar Bose (Indian born American head of Bose Corporation world Famous Sound System manufacturers). This system dispenses with conventional system by linear electro magnetic motors in each wheel. It is highly efficient and sensitive.

b. In future drives each wheel will have an electric motor and concept of front, rear and all wheel drive will disappear. Computer controlled and generated signal will operate each wheel motor according to the need.

c. Nitrogen filed tires M/s. Ingersoll Rand Co. had already developed nitrogen generator. This can be connected to any existing air compressor.

d. Infra red cameras can tell eyelid movement of driver. Whether he is fatigued or not and warn him in advance.

e. Lane departure warning, If the driver crosses the white line without advance signal driver seat will vibrate and warn the driver.

f. Alcoholkey: This will prevent drunken driver from starting the vehicle, unless he blows into a tiny tube to test his alcohol level.

g. Pop up bonnet rise up at an angle on impact.

h. Distance regulation to prevent driver from getting too close.

i. Ultrasonic parking assistance to do the job for the driver.

j. Languatronic: Language recognition instead of buttons and levers.

k. Global positioning system for guide or remote control.

Automatic brakes prevent collision: The pictures given illustrate the working of collision warning systems which operates with very high degree of accuracy. And warns the driver within few seconds.

Another picture gives an idea of employing voice technology to help the drivers to keep their eyes on the road.

Another picture gives the new generation car fitted with number of electronic sensors to monitor various systems and fore warn the driver in safe driving and correct any functional default.

Car – Acura RL – system developed by Delphi Automotive supplier. At present 6.2 Million crashes reported in US during 2004 more than 20 percent were rear impact. System uses a radar unit in the grill, which continuously monitors the rate at which the car is closing in on a vehicle ahead up to 300' away. (All actions are automatic).

* Seat backs raise to upright angle and head restraint extends putting occupant in safest position.

* Seat belts retract to remove slack and hold the passenger in place.

* Sunroof closes and steering wheel moves away from the driver.

* Seat height and angle are adjusted to keep seat belt in ideal position.

* In future models knee bolster may extend on the passenger side.

* Braking system is primed for quick reaction when driver steps on the pedal.

System likely to be introduced as standard option from 2010 onwards.

Satellite to Throttle

In 1900 air quality was not a public issue. In 2001 it has become a serious subject. It took 100 years to get here. It may take another 100 years to completely reverse.

Now 55 million vehicles are manufactured every year. About 400 million will be manufactured in the next 10 years.

Global positioning system (GPS).

First vehicle to utilize GPS Satellite system.

TMC Trucking DES MOINS IOWA.

207 Mile historic journey from US DOE KE plant to IOWA state capitol building.

In TransitAuthority of River city, 100 buses using GPS, saved 43000 gallons of fuel and reduced 11000 pounds of emission in less than one year.

Main Problems

* Over Throttling by drivers

* Aging and degradation of engine performance

* Now GPS (global positioning system) is advanced so much it is already becoming a standard fitting in most of the future vehicles

Run Flat Tire

The future model car come equipped with run flat tire that can be run without any air at all for certain distance. The side walls are reinforced. The performance of tires under zero pressure is so good that the cars must be fitted with tire pressure monitoring system that will alert the driver to the fact that he is driving on a flat tire.

Volvo safety concept car sensors locate the driver's eyes and move the seat to have better view of the road, the steering, pedals shift lever slide into easy to reach position.

Infra red cameras provide a black & white image of unlighted areas ahead video cameras watch areas where drivers cannot see such as blind spots created by hood.

Collusion alarm system activated when other vehicles comes close.

Among future fuel Hydrogen stands out as unique. The word Hydrogen is derived from Greek hydro (water) and genes (forming). So hydrogen actually means 'water forming.'

It has the density just one fourteenth of air, hydrogen does not exist as free gas on earth but it is found in over 70 percent of the substances around us. In the water we use every day, in natural gas and even in garbage. It is available in plenty. Hydrogen used to generate electricity in a fuel cell produces no harmful by products, unlike the burning of gasoline or natural gas. The only by product of spent hydrogen is water better still; this water can be used to generate more hydrogen.

In short

* Hydrogen is an extremely efficient energy source.

* It is clean.

* Can be made from a wide variety of substances.

* It can also be regenerated.

The fact, hydrogen can be regenerated from water makes it part of an endless flow, an inexhaustible energy source.

Powering vehicles with clean energy that never runs out.

Currently used a fuel in Honda FCX fuel cell electric vehicle, the car that leaves nothing behind but water.

Future developments in advanced high power braking systems, automatic transmission, suspension and electronic controls and even driverless vehicles are in the pipelines of future vehicles.

India has got first hybrid vehicle on 19th June 2008. It is a petrol-electrical version of HONDA CIVIC sedan. But it is very costly, 21.5 lakhs rupees. High cost is because of heavy import duties of 104%. It promises 47% more efficiency and less pollution. Barring the cost it is one of the best solutions to our transport related problems.

Even with such marvelous improvements. One main and notoriously unreliable link in the safety chain – The driver could not be brought in to reap the benefits.

The role of drivers will continue to remain in the forefront in future also. Awell-trained and knowledgeable driver will continue to play an all-important role, as future ideal road user.

Any of us can become the user of future vehicles. It is not in a distant future. It is very close. Some of the developments are SO CLOSE that you can touch them.

* * * * *

Automobile Air Conditioning

For heat, ventilation and air conditioning, a separate chapter is given for this subject as in future or now, no vehicle without air conditioning or climate control system is likely to be produced. It is not considered as a luxury, it is a standard fitment.

Air conditioning system was first applied to trailers for fleet operation in 1938, and in 1942 many buses were air-conditioned. In cars in early 1950, Ac was sold as standard option. It was 1.5 kilowatt refrigeration compressor located under engine hood and belt driven from crankshaft.

Automobile climate control system (CCS) is peculiar and most demanding, because

- Higher or lower temperature of outside air.

- Solar radiation and engine heat.

- The amount of heat absorbed is dependent upon.

- Automobile insulation.

- Position of sun and intensity of solar radiation.

- Variation of light and shadow.

- Vehicle color.

- Tinted glass, vehicle speed.

- Wind – direction and velocity.

Because of constantly changing external factors, maintaining the temperature, humidity, to the desired level demands a fairly sophisticated conditioning system.

In an air conditioner's refrigeration system, the refrigerant picks up the heat from the passenger compartment and is pumped to the condenser where it gives up its heat to the outside air, and then flows back to the system to pickup the heat again. The refrigerant is recycled in a closed system. The refrigerant has a good heat transfer property in the required temperature range and does not corrode system components.

During operation the refrigerant continuously changes its phase from liquid to gas and then back to liquid again. Refrigeration works on vapor (adiabatic) compression cycle, where four distinct activities such as compression, condensation, expansion (Throttling) and evaporation of the refrigerant take place. Four major components of the system responsible for four functions are

- Compressor

- Condenser

- Expansion Valve

- Evaporator

HV AC Principles

- The Air conditioning system does not manufacture cold air, but rather cools the vehicle interior by removing heat from air contained within.

- Heat always travels from an area of higher temperature to an area of lower temperature by the principle of entropy, very much like the solar heat that we get from the sun.

- The greater the difference in temperature the faster heat will flow.

- Heat will continue to flow until the temperatures of both areas become equal.

Comfort Zone

70°–80°F cooling is comfortable zone. Purpose of Air Conditioning is

- Purity

- Correct Humidity

- Efficient Circulation

- And to maintain comfortable temperature

Quick Check of Refrigerant Charge

The following procedure can be used (by owner/driver) for Quick check'whetherA/C system has a proper charge of refrigerant or not

- Run the engine at fast idle

- Operate A/C at its maximum cooling capacity

- Look at the site glass (1)

Item No./Charge of Refrigerant/Symptom/Correction

1. / Bubbles observed in sight glass / Insufficient charge / Check system for leaks

2. / No bubbles observed / No or insufficient charge / Evacuate and charge check for leaks

3. / No temperature difference between inlet and outlet / Empty or near empty system / Evacuate and charge system

4. / Noticeable temperature difference / Proper or too much charge / Discharge excess charge

5. / When A/c is turned off refrigerant in sight glass clears and remains clear / Too much charge in system / Discharge excess charge

6. / When A/c is turned off refrigerant in sight glass once produces bubbles and then clears / Proper charge of refrigerant in system / No correction required

Caution: Owner/driver never tamper with AC System. Get it attended by competent persons only.

> **Refrigerant :** HPC-1349 (R-1349)
>
> C-12 (R-12) are used.

Now constant research is going on to find more suitable non-inflammable refrigerants, which pollute less and satisfy the requirements of the end users.

Some interesting information about air conditioning systems Women tend to feel the chillness more than men.

Elderly people tend to feel the chillness more than younger people.

Slimmer people tend to feel the chillness more than fat people.

Now air conditioning systems are so advanced, that each seat in the vehicle can have it's own setting of level of air conditioning required for the occupant. Constant research is going on to improve the system to meet customers' needs.

Air conditioning system in automobiles is now more than a luxury. Not only cars most of the buses are also air conditioned and luxurious. In commercial vehicles air conditioning is widely used in transporting highly perishable goods like fish, meat, vegetables, fruits and certain drugs. They must be kept in controlled temperatures all the time to preserve their freshness.

Prudent use of air conditioning system and maintaining it periodically will increase life of all components of air conditioning system. It will also save power consumed by the system. You can enjoy the comforts with minimum or no problem. Best of all will be, at least you will be breathing unpolluted air when you are traveling in the vehicle.

Here are few useful tips to make the most efficient use of air-conditioning system in the cars

A. For faster cooling on hot days travel with windows open and ac on with fan at high position for few minutes… Then close the windows and travel with ac on recirculating mode. Then put ac in normal mode with vent closed. Set fan to slow.

B. Try to reduce the difference between out side and inside temperatures. This will reduce fuel consumption.

C. When not in use, turn on ac at least once a week to prevent, the refrigerant gas from leaking.

D. Prevent stale air caused by bacteria in the evaporator by switching off the AC 5 to 10 minutes before you leave the car. You can also plan this if you are sure of your programme and switch off ac in advance.

E. As far as possible park the vehicle in shade so that temperature difference is minimized.

An incidental advantage is that you are shielded from the outside noise created by the traffic and also of course, the dust in the air.

Medical Related Issues

One of the most stressful aspects of living in modern day life is dealing with problems that arise after an automobile accident.

There is almost no example of a truly unavoidable automobile accident. Most collisions occur because of momentary neglect or a mistake that occurs instantaneously. All such collisions are avoidable, if people would exercise proper control and not be careless.

Remember: A careless driver can strike any person at any time robbing them of their most basic and important possession their good health both physical and mental.

Most people feel dazed and confused during and after at the accident site.

Nothing is likely to test one's knowledge of first aid, more than accidents suffered on highways, injuries may be severe. You may be at great distance away from professional help. Keep this book in your car along with adequate emergency equipment.

Blankets,

Good flash lights with new Batteries

Warning lights and flares

Bandages and sterile dressing

First Aid Box

Accident is defined as absence of purpose in the succession of events. Accidents are bound to bring surprises.

In giving first aid remember that moving a victim, making a hasty attempt to get him out of the vehicle may do untold harm, particularly if there are spinal injuries or fractures are involved.

Give first aid at once inside the vehicle where possible before attempting to move the victim.

Exceptions

- When the vehicle is on fire.

- When fuel is spilled and fire hazard is great.

- When you are in a congested high speed traffic area.

- Where there is a danger of second accident to the victim.

- Follow these rules in examining the victim.

- Ensure that victim is breathing and has pulse.

- Check for hemorrhage.

- Examine for injuries particularly fractures.

First Steps in First Aid

When you approach a seriously injured patient remember ABC-

A – is for Airway makes sure the victims airway has not been blocked by tongue, secretion of saliva or some foreign body.

B – is for breathing. Make sure the person is breathing if not administer artificial respiration.

C – is for circulation. Make sure the person has pulse. If no pulse is felt administer cardio pulmonary resurrection check for bleeding.

Reassure the victim and try to remain calm. Your calmness can allay the victim's fear and panic and convince him that everything is under control.

Try to get all possible help. Here cell phone will be of great benefit always store information in case of emergency (ICE) in cell phone. Getting proper medical attention in time is very important. The first hour immediately after the accident is called the Golden hour for saving the life.

Do not force any liquids on unconscious and semi conscious persons. It may enter the windpipe and choke the person.

Now most of the places are having emergency Trauma Care Units who are working 24×7 contacting them can be of great help.

Life and death emergencies are rare. Immediate attention and proper first aid can save many persons.

It will be very useful for the readers to learn about one important First aid that would give any affected person a second life.

Cardio Pulmonary Resuscitation (CPR)

This may one of the vital first aids, which can be given to any accident victim, which is life saving. It also can be given to people who are drowned and recovered alive, and people who are suddenly having serious cardiac or respiratory attacks.

The act of administering CPR, can more than double the survival rate of victims. It will be a worthy training, which any one can undergo under proper training establishments like hospitals, St John Ambulance centers or any notified NGOS. You will be proud of such training, as you will be able to save many lives.

How to Do It

The Two Step Method

1. Call for ambulance or emergency medical assistance and rush back to the victim

2. If the victim shows no movement, check if he/she is breathing. If there is no sign of breathing, let the person lie down with chin facing up. Put your hands on the center of the chest and press. Keep pumping the chest for at least 100 times a minute till you see positive signs or till medical help arrives

Three Step CPR

1. Call for emergency medical assistance or for an ambulance and rush back to victim.

2. If the victim shows no movement, check his/her breathing. If there is no breathing, let the person lie down with chin facing up. Tilt the head back and listen to breathing. If the victim is not breathing normally, pinch nose and cover the mouth with yours and blow until you see the chest rise. Give two breaths; each breath should take one second.

3. Put your hands on the center of the chest and press. Keep pumping the chest at least 100 times a minute till the person responds or till help arrives.

Special Note for Treating Children

When the victim-is-a child (between 1 and 8 years) CPR should be given for two minutes before calling medical attention. Use only hands do not put your body weight. Use very gentle force but keep number of pumps to 100 per minute. For infants use just three fingers below the nipple for compression give mouth-to-mouth respiration also.

As per the recent study of American heart association, the chest compressions are enough to save adults who collapse during cardiac arrests. Compressions make the heart beat again and leading to the revival of blood circulation and delay the death of tissue.

Scenario Immediately after the Accident

The victims and others feel dazed and confused.

They may ask

Am I ok?

Are my passengers (if any) ok?

What is the condition of my car?

Oh I wonder if the other person is ok?

Who is at fault?

For the time being your life has not changed.

After about 5 days or so, you start feeling you are not your normal self. You may feel:

Muscle stiffness

Neck pain

Numbness and tingling

Mild back pain, low back pain

Difficulty in sleeping

Instability, memory loss

Fatigue, difficulty in concentrating

Spasms

Headaches

Or Worse

You may be injured and feel nothing at all. Injured people feel less injured under influence of medications.

Hidden Injury

A lot of automobile accident victims receive inappropriate care from hospitals and medical centers, or physical therapy clinics. The pain or damages are hidden or numbed with drug.

Whiplash occurs when the head and neck are thrown or snapped back and forth very quickly at speed as slow as 5 Mph (8 Kmph). **The amount of damage to the automobile bears little relationship, to the force applied to the cervical neck** (**spine of the occupants.** In other words the severity of injury to passengers or other persons is not necessarily directly related to the damage to the vehicle. It will be very difficult to convince the insurance people on this point.

The neck is jam packed with nerves, glands, tubes, blood vessels, lymph modes and 48 different joints. Add to that your brain stem, spinal column, disk muscle, tendons, ligament fluids, meningitis and more.

The chances of one becoming a whiplash victim in an accident are extremely high.

In case of two wheeler drivers and pillion riders driving without helmets, injury can be fatal because of skull injury. Helmets will offer live saving safety and there is no compromise on safety without helmets. Majority of the fatal accidents in two wheelers are due to non-wearing of helmets. Even best possible medical attention given immediately cannot reduce or offset, the severity of damage, which is likely to result in permanent disability if not death.

The real first aid for two wheeler users is only helmet. There should be no element of doubt about wearing helmet in the minds of all two-wheeler users. It is a question of their own safety.

Therefore proper medical examination by competent medical authorities is a must. To restore oneself to original health after an accident is an extremely painful and long drawn process and require lots of money and time. Safe guarding your interest is very important.

The purpose of insurance is precisely to provide financial relief to the aggrieved persons. That is why it has been made compulsory for third party. It will be definitely wise to cover all aspects by paying the required premium. Compared to the benefits by way of compensation and reimbursement of repair charges etc, the premium paid is just a pittance.

Of course the best policy is no accidents, no claims, but coverage is full for all eventualities.

All medical related issues are having legal implications, so keeping all records and policies in force are vital.

Normally getting payments from insurance is a really tough job.

Consumer organizations, courts, free legal advices. Ombudsmen are available for redressal. Remember any injured person require lots of money and time for recovering to original health immediately after the accident. Meanwhile your earning capacity will be affected considerably.

Knowing all formalities is very important. The purpose of this book is to educate the readers the necessity to have a thorough knowledge. Dealing each type of accident will be different. It is absolutely necessary to get all legal, medical assistance through the agencies dealing with them. Whether you are a third party involved in an automobile accident or a driver, passenger of an automobile you are entitled to proper medical treatment and financial compensation. Both are vital for post accident recovery.

Remember

A. Whether you are a vehicle owner or driver, always ensure you are having all necessary documents like valid driving license for the type of vehicle you are driving

B. Always ensure your insurance coverage is adequate and valid at all times

C. Carry the essential medical emergency kits with you always particularly when you are traveling on highways and long distances

D. Undergo training on first aid, cardio pulmonary Resuscitation and how to provide emergency treatments in case of accidents

E. Become members of the associations like AAI, AASI, MYTVS etc which will provide emergency assistance in case of unfortunate accidents

F. Have information about various government and non government agencies which are listed for rendering assistance in case of emergencies

Last, but not the least, read and reread the pledge you have given in the beginning of the book and ensure you give all possible help and assistance to the needy. This will be one of best services you will be rendering to humanity.

Motor Vehicles Act and Rules

Transport related problems existed much before the invention of Automobiles.

This can be seen from the following.

Hence forward, no wheeled vehicles, whatsoever will be allowed within the precincts of the city, from sunrise until the hour before dark.

Those, which shall have entered (During night and still within the city at dawn) must halt and stand empty until the appointed hour.

– Senatus consultum of JULIUS CEASER 44 BC

It is absolutely impossible to sleep anywhere in the city. The perpetual traffic of wagons in the narrow winding streets is sufficient to wake the dead.

(The satires of Juvenal) AD 117.

Everyone who lived in the earth much before us, were also facing transport related problems may be on a lesser degree than ours. The necessity for enacting laws was there. Now they are more pronounced.

Motor vehicles act and rules are known as All India Motor Vehicles act and rules and applicable throughout India, It was originally formulated in 1939, during British Rules and amended from time to time.

Automobile technology in India was mainly on borrowed terms from various countries. Initially it was from UK for standard, Hindustan Motors for Cars and Ashok Leyland for commercial vehicles and Royal Enfield for Motor Cycles.

Fiat and Vespa (now Bajaj) from Italy and Tata from Germany. The real water shed on Automobile Industry was from 1983, when Maruti Cars were started to be produced. Only around 40000 cars including two wheelers were sold in a year. Now more than a million vehicles are being sold every year. Prior to that cars were more of a luxury and taxed heavily. There was not much of significant technology inAutomobiles, Roads, and Ancillaries etc.

The Motor Vehicles Act with a few amendments was found satisfactory. But with liberalized policies on transport industry as a whole saw huge development. Now India is having more than 6 crore vehicles and 33 lacs kilometers of Road.

All changes necessitated extensive revision of the Motor Vehicles Act. The latest act is known as motor vehicle (amendment bill 2017 and 2018) and has 14 chapters (217 sections) and a schedule, which gives various traffic signs.

Power of LicensingAuthority to disqualify and hold the license (for commercial vehicles).

1. Assaults on Passengers

2. Theft of personal effects of passengers

3. Transport of goods prohibited by law

4. Abduction of passengers

5. Over load

6. Exceeding posted speed limits

7. Failure to stop when ordered by authorities

8. Misbehavior to passengers

9. Abandoning of Vehicles in public places normally or after an accident

10. Driving under the influence of liquor or drug

11. Demanding on citing excessive fare by a driver of Motor Cab

12. Using mobile or cell phone while driving

13. Not accepting the first offer by Motor Cab Driver

Some of the important chapters, which must be known to all, are given below with brief notes against each chapter.

Chapter IV: Registration of Motor Vehicles displayed

No vehicle can be driven unless it is registered and their registration marks is displayed in prescribed manner. For example in commercial vehicles it should be displayed in front and rear and both sides. prescribed form should be filled and vehicle must be produced before registering authority. The registration certificate will indicate the engine, chassis no and ownership details. It is valid throughout India for 15 years and can be renewed for 5 years. In case vehicle is plying in another state for period exceeding six months it should be registered fresh in new state.

Chapter II: Driving License – issue of

No person can drive a vehicle in any public place unless he holds the valid driver license for the particular vehicle. A person may drive motorcycle without gear after attaining the age of 16 years; for all other cases the person should be above 18 years of age.

For obtaining a License

a. A person should be above 18 Years.

b. Must be in sound health and should be certified by a doctor for fitness to drive.

c. Must obtain a learner license and after completing one month after learners license he/she can appear for driving test.

d. The validity of license is 3 years for heavy vehicles and five to 20 years for cars depending on the age of the driver.

e. The driving license must be renewed within 30 days of expiry.

Chapter VII

Construction and maintenance of motor vehicles. Every motor vehicle shall be so constructed and maintained, as to be at all times under the effective control of person driving the vehicle.

Chapter VIII

Control of traffic No Vehicle can be driven at a public place at a speed exceeding maximum speed for the vehicle fixed by authorities and notified.

No vehicle should exceed the permissible load.

All drivers should obey all traffic signs. This is both mandatory and cautionary.

All motor vehicles should be kept in good working condition.

No vehicle should be parked or abandoned in such a position or condition as likely to cause danger or inconvenience to other road users.

All two wheeler drivers and pillion riders must wear protective headgears.

In case a vehicle or vehicles involved in an accident the driver and others in the vehicles should take all reasonable steps to secure medical assistance, including taking then to nearest hospital.

Report the incident at the nearest police station (First Information Report) as soon as possible, in any case within twenty-four hours of the occurrence.

Chapter XI

Insurance of motor vehicles against third party risk. No person can drive a vehicle in public place unless there is in force in relation to the use of the vehicle by that person, a policy of insurance against third party risk.

In case of transfer of ownership of the vehicle to another person, the insurance policy shall also be deemed to have been transferred, in favor of the buyer. The new owner has to apply for the insurance within fourteen days from the date of transfer for making necessary changes in the owner's name.

The Transport authority can detain your vehicle, for the following:

1. Driving without valid license.

2. Driving unregistered motor vehicle.

3. Non-payment of motor vehicle taxes.

4. Rash or negligent driving.

5. Driving under influence of alcohol & drugs.

6. Without valid insurance coverage for third party risk.

You can be penalized by RTO for the following:

1. Exceeding the permissible speed limit (sec 112)

2. Not obeying traffic rules and regulations (sec 118, 119, 121)

3. Leaving or parking vehicle in a dangerous position (Sec 122)

4. Riding on running board or on top or on the bonnet of vehicle (Sec 123)

5. Not wearing helmet while riding on two wheeler (sec 129)

6. Carrying more than one person in addition to the driver on two wheeler motor cycle (sec 128)

7. Talking on cell/mobile phone while driving (MMr Rule 250-a)

8. Failure to produce driving license and certificate of registration insurance to the officer on duty (sec 130)

Various provisions of the motor vehicles act are given not for any legal objective in view (for which the readers should refer the original act and take proper legal counsel) but only as general information.

The purpose is to emphasize the importance of legal aspects, which must be borne in mind always. This will indirectly induce safety consciousness in all Road users.

The third schedule sec 7–6 and 17–6. Test for competence to drive. The candidate shall satisfy the person conducting the test that he/she is able to:

1. Start the engine of the vehicle

2. Move away straight ahead and at an angle while at the same time engaging the first and intermediate gears until top gear is reached.

3. To change down to lower gear quickly from top gear when traffic conditions warrant such change.

4. Overtake or allow to be overtaken, meet the path of other vehicles and take appropriate course and precaution, giving appropriate signals.

5. Turn left and right and then course correctly.

6. Stop the vehicle in an emergency and normally and in the later bring it to rest at an appropriate course of the road.

7. Drive the vehicle backwards and while doing so enter limited openings to the right or left.

8. Cause the vehicle to face opposite direction by means of forwards and reverse gears.

9. By hand and mechanical signals in a clear and unmistakable manner appropriate signals at appropriate times to indicate their intended action.

10. Act correctly and promptly on all signals and other road users signals.

11. Demonstrate general control of the vehicle, by confidently steering and smooth gear changing and braking as and when necessary.

12. To change quickly to lower gear while driving down hill.

13. To stop and restart the vehicle on a steep upward incline making proper use of hand brake, throttle and foot brake without any rolling back.

Test No. 13, is undoubtedly the toughest as it requires total undivided concentration and skill of the driver.

In addition they should be conversant with general traffic rules and regulations and capable of handling emergencies. Proper eyesight and hearing and understanding meanings of various signs.

Since 2000 Road Lengths has increased by 39%, No of vehicles has increased by 158%, 78% of Accidents are caused by errant drivers due to over speeding and Drunken Driving.

Motor vehicle act amendment bill in 2017 and 2018 dealt with all issues with positive note. It is learnt that more than 6–7 crores vehicles are running without any insurance. They all must be identified and brought into insurance ambit.

But law alone won't solve the problems. There should be social movement to address the root cause of problems of over speeding, Drunken Driving and pedestrian safety and use of Helmets etc., Then only we can achieve some tangible results.

So our motto drive safe and be safe should spread far and wide and will defenitely bring results.

Mind You: Nearly anyone of sound mind and body can learn to drive a car-vehicle, But to drive safely and well with consideration. It is an art, and only begins when driving test is over.

* * * * *

Policeman to motorist: You are driving at 65 kilometers per hour, and speed limit is 50 kilometers per hour.

Motorist: No, I was driving only at 50 kilometers per hour.

They started arguing.

Motorist's wife intervened and told the policeman not to argue with her husband when he is drunk.

Interesting Facts

Nowhere in the world the car with two over lapping black RR on the radiator goes unrecognized. It is the great Rolls Royce.

FREDERIK HENRY ROYCE and HONORABLE CHARLES S. ROLLS formed the company with an aim to eliminate every possible flaw in every part of the machine before it was produced In 1904 after a year of grueling work first the prototypes were produced. It had two cylinder 10 horsepower. When engine is running one can neither hear nor feel. In 1907 rolls arranged a demo, which proved the car's reputation for all times. It was almost nonstop, 15000 miles, 48 day running from LONDON TO GLASGOW and back on road, which is used in, to day's brutal testing tracks.

The car was then handed over to mechanics of royal automobile club with instructions to strip the vehicle totally and replace any part which is not as good as factory new. Their repair bill, regrinding of valves and replacing water pump amounted to 2 pounds 2 shillings and 7 pence (about Rs. 135/in today's rate) their motto – was 'whatever is rightly done, however humble is noble.'

AMERICAN: Most obsessed people luxurious lazily powerful. Never minded about fuel consumption (not now) sports utility vehicles.

EUROPEONS: Smaller cars because or lack of space.

BRITISH: The best car in the world Rolls Royce Silver Ghost. Sought after by Maharajas, Billionaires.

GERMANS: First practical car were all stainless steel and top class engineering. Rock solid great to drive for 100 years.

ITALIAN: Highly emotional prone to tantrums. Screaming fast Best looking cars. Ferrari and Alfa Romeo.

FRENCH: Pioneer in auto technology. Rocket science technology in car.

JAPAN: Shrinking every thing. Cars never brake down for 100000 miles. Never needed petrol (incredibly cheap) 10 times cheaper. Now Korea offers cheaper cars.

INDIANS: We are the masters of borrowed technology. At present the fastest growing auto giant in motor vehicles and component industry.

1. **Longest Car:** 100' long with 26 wheels/include a swimming pool with dive board.

2. **Biggest Car:** Bugatti royale Tie 41. Assembled in France in 1927 eight cylinder 2.5 gallon engine 22 feet long engine hood 7.1 feet long.

3. **Lightest Car:** Built and driven by Louvis Bonni of London, weighing 21 lbs 25cc engine max speed 15 MPH.

4. **Most Valued G.M Model Car:** GM prowler value $210000 (Rs. 9.5 Crores) for Chrsyler Plymouth inauguration made of 15000 carrot amethyst and 19 lbs of white gold wind shield made out of Rock crystal.

5. **Biggest Private Rolls Royce Fleet:** Sultan Hassamal Bokiab of Bruni 150 Rolls Royce fleet.

6. **Longest Road Bridge:** Second lake of PONCHATRAM. Joining Manderilla and Metraive Louisiana 23 miles 1538 yards long.

7. **Highest Motorable Road in the world:** INDIA KHARDUGLA PASS KASHMIR at highest point climbs 5656.82 Meters (18640 feet). Built by Border Roads Organization India in 1976, and opened for vehicular traffic in 1988.

8. **Lowest Road:** The world's lowest road runs along ISRALI shores of the Dead Sea at 393 Meters (1289 feet) below sea level completed in 1958.

9. **Longest Ring Road:** 121.8 miles M-25 London Airbital motor way six lanes UK completed on October 29, 1986. Cost 1333 Million Pounds. 7 Million dollars per kilometer.

10. **Largest Bus fleet:** Andhra Pradesh Road Transport Corporation. They have 18397 buses operating in 8745 routes.

11. **Longest Bus:** Articulated DAP Super Train Buses CANGO 105-feet long carries 350 Passengers.

12. **Earliest Bus:** First municipal motor omnibus of the world inaugurated on April 12, 1903. Ran between east Bourne Railway Station and MEADS EAST – SUSSEX UK.

13. **Longest Trucks on Public Roads:** 175.5 feet long and weighs 125 Tons Australian Road Train.

14. **Largest Tire:** Standing 13'1 "tall weighing 4 Ton. Built by Michlin to fit special dump truck caterpillar's largest model 797.

15. **Largest Dump Truck:** T-282 Lrebhem mining equipment co Virginia USA. Pay load 327 Tons 47'6" long 28'7" wide and 24' high, weighs 201 Ton.

16. **Highest Car Mileage:** 1960 Valvo P-l800f owned by IRVEM GORDUM of USA. He reached 2 Million miles (3.2 million KM) on March, 7, 2002 in NBC studio times square New York.

17. **Most Fuel-efficient Vehicle:** Best fuel consumption ever recorded 10240 miles per gallons, (3624.5 Km) per liter). Tear Fancy CANUL NOK JAPAN, in Scottish Marathon onAugust 12, 2001.

18. **Longest Car Pileup on films:** The climax of film Blue brother 2000, marked by a car chase resulting in pile up involved 50 CARS. The crash sequence lasted over just 2 minutes in film. But it took four months to film.

19. **Smallest Car:** PSO Peal engineering Co Isle of Man in 1966. It was 4'5" long and 3.25 feet wide 4'5" inches height weight 132 lbs.

20. **Heaviest Car:** Soviet built 21 liter 12.75 feet wheel base, weight 3.02 tons used by Mikolai Gorbachev till December 1991. Eight-cylinder engine guzzled 6 miles per gallon.

21. **Sales Pitch:** Wishing to sell a car, the car was parked in front of the office and owner left an ad on the rear window which read.

'Searching for a new master. My name is MIRCAI am from a family of Nissan in the land of rising sun.

According to my master, I have always been 'one who never failed.' Still she decided to trade me for a new one. Who ever want me; I will keep my promise of being a faithful slave. In return I only demand to be well treated, as I have always been.

Within half an hour the car was sold.

* * * * *

Some Amazing Facts about Honda Car

22. World Record fuel efficient in 1996 Honda Dolphin, an amazingly fuel efficient vehicle established a new world record on one liter of fuel at the shell mileage marathon in Finland, by achieving 3337 Kilometer braking the existing record of 2687 Kilometer set in 1992.

23. Hi-tech Honda dream car won the 1996Australian World Solar challenge Race, by traveling from Darwin to Adelaide in a record 33.32 hours. This time shattered the record of previous winner, 1993-dream car by more than two hours. 1996 dream car was the first two person solar car to win this race making a record average speed of 28.76 Kmph.

24. The world's first engine to pass California ULTRA low emission vehicle standards. It was the first engine, by incorporating variable valve timing and lift electronic-control, with extremely lean mixture, harmful emissions are cut by about 90% while retaining the same power, torque and fuel efficiency as a standard unit.

25. The first car to be manufactured in India was Hindustan 10 by Hindustan Motors Kolkatta.

26. First parking meter was installed in USA Oklahoma City in 1930.

Cutting edge engine technology.

1. Valves without camshaft. Double acting solenoids by Siemens.

2. Common rail fuel injection system with electronically controlled injectors.

3. Spark to piston earth electrode fitted on high point of piston instead of in spark plug 'Saab' had developed an engine like this.

4. Variable compression and valve timing. Using hinge point aid tilting cam both high and low compression are obtained.

New Products

1. Long life spark plugs auto light titanium spark plugs coated with anti seize on the threads for easy removal and installation.

   1,00,000 miles (1,60,000 Km) without replacement. Double titanium tips for No Gap erosion.

2. Leak finder traces product with 12 volts blue Ultra violet bulbs and florescent dye for adding to oil and coolant. To identify leakages even if it is hairline cracks.

3. Infrared Thermometer. This can be used for engine troubleshooting, climate control system repairs, and brake

system inspection, tire alignment monitoring cooling system.

4. Pressure cooker Cool charges with a properly sized super charge and custom programmed ECM that corrects air fuel ratio, ignition and injection timing and transmission shift point.

    Easy to install kit. Increases HP by 55% and torque by 41%.

5. Air Fare (?): Air cleaner molded from high poly utherane including a pre oiled high flow air filter.

Power from Peanut

Future power source. System designed byAtlartic University and funded by Georgia University. Uses high-pressure steam to reduce papery peanut shells to carbon and hydrogen. Carbon for water and hydrogen for engine. In both case the exhaust is virtually pure water.

* * * * *

King Midget was delivered in a crate, can be assembled in a garage. All state legal car cylinder air-cooled Wisconsin engine weighted 550 pounds 50 Mph speed. 80 miles per gallon, chain driven Base price 560 dollars.

Plastics in car

10% reduction in weight will reduce 5% on fuel consumption. With 15 million vehicles, it will make appreciable difference. Lot of components is made from plastics and fiberglass.

Special Testing

Toyota V8 engine tested at 10000 RPM for 20 hours continuously. Assume the stroke be 100 mm – 3.93." Distance traveled by piston in each revolution is 200 mm (20 cm).

(Distance traveled in one minute).

20 cm × 10000 = 2,00,000 cm

2000 meter/2 Km

In one hour 2 × 60 = 120 Km

In 20 hours 120 × 20 = 2400 Km at average speed of 120 Km per hour and coming to dead stop 20000 times every minute. This is to give an idea of tremendous strain the components are subject to.

* * * * *

In Washington, a motorist with criminal intention is required to stop at city limits and telephone to police chief to inform him that he is entering the town

* * * * *

In 1960, GM'S CORVAIR, was declared as 'UNSAFE AT ANY SPEED,' because the engine was in the rear.

* * * * *

Women customers are more demanding than men. Even on performance. Safety, mechanical ability not much of difference between male and female driver. Driving skills are similar.

But woman drivers are safe. Their all time driving ability is limited.

* * * * *

Car Use

In USA 90% of people are traveling by own car. 70% of people travel alone for work or shopping.

Average cost of keeping a car monthly is around $703 for 30 hours every month

Sharing with others, monthly cost will be $3.50 to $10.00

* * * * *

LONDON transport company had saved around 120000 pounds (Rs. 98 lacs) in their maintenance and running costs by following a novel lubrication technique.

As per auto magazine 'Commercial transport' by using castor oil as lubricant in rear axles of their buses, they could reduce fuel consumption by about 2 to 3% without compromising of efficiency of the fleet. Using castor oil as lubricant, the friction was reduced and this in turn increased life of components. By adding oxidation inhibitors the stickiness of castor oil was reduced.

This is a real food for thought for our fleet operators.

* * * * *

Every year, 50,000,000 automobiles are produced in the world.

In 2002, the most popular color of the car, in north America was silver.

The most recycled product in the world is the automobiles.

As per the recent recommendations of parliament committee:

Any drunken driver commits a fatal accident, his action will not be constructed as due to mere negligence; it will be treated as a premeditated crime and he/she is likely to be punished under section 304 of the ipc which deals with pre mediated crime. To safe guard the interests of the accident victims a portion of the third party liability premium collected from all vehicles will be put in a corpus of the solatium fund. Minimum compensation for death due to accidents should be Rs. One lath and Rs. 50000 for grievous injuries This is a definite and positive step to alleviate the grievances of accident victims.

* * * * *

Real Life Incidents

This chapter contains lots of real life incidents. Some have happy and delightful endings and some have very unhappy and sad endings. I can vouch that none of the incidents were foreseen or welcomed by the affected persons. Still they were caused, by some unintentional neglect or error.

In most of the cases the affected persons did not have any connection, with the events preceding the accident. They suffered for no fault of theirs.

I sincerely hope the readers will seriously introspect all incidents and learn life saving lessons. Not only we should learn the lessons, but also we should pass the life saving lessons to all around us. By this we will be rendering valuable service to the present and future generations.

Stolen Car found after 37 years.

Scene 1

Alan poster – 26 years guitar salesman from Brooklyn New York native moved from Queens to a 21st street studio in Chealsea.

He bought a blue corvette 1968 Model.

Jan 21, 1969 – Attempted by somebody to steal the vehicle. Foiled, but he let the man go and did not report the incident.

Jan 22, 1969 – Next night the car was stolen. Within 22 days, poster's car was the 6620th car to be stolen in the year 1969. Total of 78000 cars had been stolen during the entire year 1969.

Scene 2

December 2005 – After 37 years. Routine check by two New York detectives casually stopped the car for identification. It confirmed to the police report of January 22, 1969. More than a miracle the car survived and was in good running condition and was supposed to have been shipped to Sweden at a fairly good price.

Now – Best Part of the story

Most interesting point is that the car was not insured against theft as Mr. Poster (Owner) could not afford it. What a fantastic luck...!

* * * * *

Details of a typical legal case tried by Wisconsin (USA) Supreme Court.

Tire related accident in 1991.

High Lights:

1. Vehicle Volkswagen vanagan.

2. Fitted with continental tires – wrong selection.

3. Brought from tire dealer two years, prior to accident tire was 10 years old at the time of selling.

4. Tire pressure was never checked.

5. Three months earlier, the snow tires, which were fitted, were found to be over-inflated by 25% above recommended pressure.

6. The car was having dad, mom, children, luggage and one sailboat on the roof and one boat trailing behind in tow.

7. Both mom & dad had worked full shift previous day before starting.

8. Journey started on previous day at 6 P.M.

9. 23 hours drive on snow tires.

10. The vehicles, was traveling at 72 MPH when it hit a dip.

11. Sleep deprived mom, who was driving, slowed down the car from 72 MPH to 40 MPH by driving for a distance of several hundred yards.

12. The car flipped over.

13. She was paralyzed.

Case was filed against the tire company by the injured couple.

Judgment: The jury concluded that 'continental' the tire maker was strictly liable for the accident. (i.e.) the tire has been in an unreasonably dangerous condition, from the moment they left the factory 12 years ago.

How so? Because continental had installed a nylon cap over the belt assembly-to discourage belt separation. (Which was the cause of accident). So obviously it must have known the tires were prone to belt reparation.

Award. $ 12 million dollar as compensation.

* * * * *

Famous fire stone wilderness.

Tire recall.

Firestone wilderness tires 17" fitted in ford explorer sports utility vehicle.

Recall: 6.5 Million tires in first recall

13 Million tires in second recall

Cost: $ 3 Billion US dollars.

Failure sequence:

1. The tire ply gets separated and is filling the well of the wheel rim.

2. This locks movement of one wheel.

3. The driver tries to control the vehicles, but the vehicle topples.

The main issue is tire pressure.

Fire stone company recommendation	30
PSI Ford recommendation	26 PSI

4PSI difference in tire in tire pressure brings center of gravity down by 0.99 inches.

Certified speed	110 MPH

Accident death 203 till recall.

Point of Argument:

Whether the tire design is defective or vehicle design is defective.

Very interesting case of phenomenal recalls and clashes of giants.

The relationship for 97 years ended.

* * * * *

One girl of 18 years driving a Maruthi car ran over a watchman in Kesavaperumal puram (Raja Annanialaipuram Chennai-28). The girl did not have license to drive the car. She had been arrested on manslaughter charges released on bail, awaiting trial.

This is a clear case of avoidable accident. None of those involved wanted the accident. It just added on to the fatality list due to road accidents.

Imagine the family members of the watchman.

* * * * *

When Mr. Rajaji was chief Minister of Chennai (Madras) he was traveling in his car to the central station. The policeman on duty put down his hand and traffic moved in all directions, preventing Rajaji's car from entering the station.

Rajaji coolly got down from the car and walked to the Railway Station. The station Master, learning about this, came running and informed Rajaji "He could have stopped the train for Rajaji."

Rajaji replied "You should not do it for any one person, whoever he may be."

Police also arrived, profusely apologizing for policeman's carelessness. Again Rajaji replied "No, the policeman is a normal human being." He also uttered one of wisest slogan.

"Policeman's hand is law's hand. It must be respected."

Just compare it with today's scenario in any of the roads/cities.

* * * * *

Industrialist Vijayan of Chennai went to Pondichery on 09.04.2006. While returning from Pondichery, his vehicle was hit by a Maruthi van from behind. Petrol tank of his car broke and petrol leaked out and vehicle caught fire. Neighbors came and helped and he escaped with their help.

Saturday 10 June 2006

Place: Alwarpet Fly Over

Pavithra aged 22 years, was riding her scooter, with one pillion rider. They were climbing the over bridge and over speeding. The scooter hit the railing and both of them fell down on the car, which was coming on the road below and then fell on the road. Pavithra died in the accident and other pillion rider seriously injured.

The accident could have been avoided. It occurred because of over speeding and both of them were not wearing helmets.

* * * * *

Date of time: July 2002 night 11 P.M.

Place: Phoenix – Arizona USA

Three persons traveling in a car were waiting at a traffic signal. When it turned green, ignoring cardinal principle of not assuming the right of way, they gunned their vehicle.

A drunken driver going at 65 Kmph ran the red light and slammed into driver's side. The driver, 17 years old Para was injured seriously.

All the ligaments supporting the 17 years old head has been severed. His skull was literally detached from his spine. Only his neck muscles kept the head connected to the body. Miraculously there was no bleeding. He was taken to St. Joseph's Hospital and Medical Center. That night neuro surgeon Curtis Dickman happened to be on call.

What followed afterwards is a medical history.

Mobility was key. The spines greatest flexibility is centered at the first and second vertebrae of the neck. That is where the head pivots normally the vertebrates are joined by fusion, preventing pivoting of the head.

Dr. Dockman and his assistant Gonzales tried an entirely new approach. Normally most of such cases result in death on the spot. Only 15 cases worldwide proved to be partial success in such injuries.

The daring new approach was to drive screws through Parra's spine and fix spine vertebrae and skull. He would have become the first person to undergo this experimental technique. The surgeons drilled two holes through first vertebrae and base of the skull. Next he inserted metal guide wire into the holes and pulled both bone-surfaced wires, which he removed slowly and carefully tightening the screws. It was a good. It was ok a bone graft had healed perfectly.

Now he can be normal except he cannot turn his head all the way in one direction.

You value everything you have, because it could all be gone in a second.

The lesson is a drunk driver had done so much damage, even though he had no intention. The drink played the devil's role.

Medical profession's excellence and daring deed of neuro surgeon Curtis Dickman saved the life.

Honest Question: 'Was not the entire incident avoidable?'

* * * * *

First Known Traffic Violation

It is recorded that one pioneer motorist Heny Hewetson, after he had been warned by police for not carrying a red flag in front of his car, took advantage of the loophole in the 1865 Act. The act did not specify any particular size of the flag. He had his son precede him bearing a banner made of ordinary pencil to which was attached a bit of quarter inch red ribbon. The speed of the car was around 2.5 miles per hour. It was not a violation of traffic rules.

* * * * *

My Car Won't Stop

A car that was running normally got in serious problem of charging into speed, not allowing the driver to reduce the speed or change down the gear.

The vehicle clocked up to 177 Kmph. The driver had to travel for 64 minutes traveled 183 Km before coming to a stop, by entering a median 8.5 meter wide and somersaulting to a halt after crashing into a truck.

Miraculously the driver did not hit any car or injured anybody. She had only superficial injury. Mechanical inspection of the car revealed a loose bolt in the transmission. The bolt got stuck and not allowed the driver to change the gear or decelerate the vehicle.

* * * * *

For No Fault of Hers

November 1968,
Time 2.30 P.M.

Her car was hit by a truck on a snowy road. First the people around thought she was dead. But she survived. Emergency treatment involved orthopedic, obstetric, general surgery, plastic and dental and every specialist of the hospital was called in to join in the operations.

She underwent more than 35 plastic surgeries over a period of next seven years.

All for no fault of hers.

John Justin lost a leg when an MTC bus lost control and drove into the wrong side of the road. It is a typical case where neither MTC driver nor John Justin wanted to be part of accident. Fate decided otherwise.

The real story of trauma and agony began like this. At the prime age of 40 at the time of accident (now he is 49), with two young children and wife to support, his agony with the loss of one leg and damaged wrist is still continuing.

He was treated in Apollo Hospital, but MMTC had not cleared his bills. Justin had to file in High court for a compensation of Rs. 12 lacks from MTC.

No compensation could be enough. But timely relief could at least make his life livable. Many meet with same or similar fate on the roads every day. While very few of them get a fair deal, most of them live with the agony life long.

* * * * *

Trauma of an Accident Victim

Ms. Mohana (age 40 years) a poor woman married to a rickshaw puller, trying to stand on her feet – literally for she was yet another accident victim. The auto rickshaw in which she was traveling toppled after hitting a rubble in the median in Rajaji Salai, Chennai around 10.30 P.M. on August 19, 2001. She was taken to Stanley Hospital and then transferred to General Hospital because of her severe head injury. The accident occurred in an accident-prone area. She had to wait for a long time for expert opinion from neurologist and orthopedic the accident had made her life miserable for years without any help or relief coming from any source.

Accident should be viewed as socio-economic problem as they made a severe impact on the entire family and livelihood. We have a long way to go in dealing with post accident problems.

This Incident Occurred Near the Vadapalani Bus Stand

An omni bus coming on hundred feet road did not stop at traffic signals and ran over and killed 3 persons for no fault of theirs. The reason given during investigation was that the driver pressed the accelerator instead of brakes.

* * * * *

The following are miracles, which were witnessed by the author personally.

One: Place Jodhpur – one night in June 1979.

Mechanic Jodha Singh of Border roads organization was traveling in a bus from Barmer to Jodhpur in night. He kept his right hand out of the window and was fast asleep.

Another truck coming from opposite direction crushed his right hand with multiple fractures. He was admitted in civil Hospital Jodhpur. They were preparing to amputate his hand. Fortunately he could phone the author at 2 o'clock in night. The author got him out of civil Hospital and admitted him in Military Hospital, Jodhpur.

He was twice lucky; the duty doctor at 3 A.M. was an orthopedic. The doctor examined him, and as no gangrene was set, he was kept under observation for two days. His hand was not amputated. But he had to undergo physiotherapy in Military Hospital, Delhi for six months before he could become near normal.

Two: Place Dorranga in Bhutan foothills.

A chilly night in February 1970. Mechanic Sardara Singh who was traveling in a Nissan Jonga was hit by the front door edge when he fell down from the vehicle, as the door got suddenly opened. Apparently there was no external injury. But in a few hours he developed severe pain in stomach and had to be hospitalized. He was declared dangerously ill as he could not pass urine. Fortunately, for him a helicopter was available and he was evacuated to the military Hospital, Tezpur (Assam). From there he was further evacuated to command Hospital, Calcutta by military Aircraft.

There an emergency major surgery was performed to clear his urinary system. He is well and energetic now.

Some Weird Facts

Mr. Peter of Australia was filming a safety program on operation of forklifts. During filming he drove the fork life across the yard and was thrown out of the forklift and was crushed to death. He did not wear his seat belt as required for safety. He drove faster than normal speed recommended on a gravel road.

New Mexico January 25, 2001

An unidentified eighteen-year-old boy died in a freak accident. He was riding a scooter without helmet and carrying a bottle of liquor and, wearing dark clothes in the night. His scooter was accidentally clipped with side view minor of a pickup truck and he died after hitting the street.

Out with a Bang April, 19, 2000 Georgia

Robert, a mechanic was welding a tractor wheel rim without deflating the tire. The air inside the tire and water moisture inside the tire was heated up and finally exploded and killed the Mechanic.

* * * * *

I Am the Driver Who Killed My Son

Day October, 14, 1994 Time 6.02 P.M. Father driving the car with his beloved son, but with blood alcohol level of 0.14 percent not to mention of anti depressant ZANON.

His son was playing with plastic robot dropped one on the floor. Father bent down to pick it up. Vehicle swerved over the centerline and hit the vehicle coming from opposite direction. His son was looking at him when he died.

He pleaded guilty in the court, to a manslaughter charge for his son's death.

How do you punish yourself for killing your own child? Father tells 'every time you take a drink and get behind the wheel you become a potential killer.'

Moral of the story is a father who adored his son became his killer. It is not he, but the drinks he took that did the job.

* * * * *

Mumbai December 9, 2005 Friday Evening

This is a typical incident with lots of positive points.

Bollywood actor Saif Ali's land cruiser car hit a 13 year old boy Shakel Shaikh.

The boy, resident of Gilbert hill, Andheri (west) suffered a fracture to his left leg. Actor Saif Ali was driving. He was checked for blood alcohol level found no alcohol in blood.

Saif himself took the injured to Arogya Nidhi Hospital and then informed police. He had also spoken to the family of the boy agreed to bear all medical expenses.

Saif was booked under section 338 of IPC causing grievous hurt by endangering life of personal safety of others, released on bail on a bond of Rs. 5,000/-

* * * * *

Chennai, November 20, 2005

Student of class VII of P.S. Senior School, Mylapore, Sri Vijaya Madhavan died in an accident in Venkatakrishna Iyer Road, Madaveli. He was riding a bicycle and was ran over by a MTC Bus.

It is not enough if we obey the traffic rules. We must be sharp in observing traffic around us. Make allowances for other's mistakes. That is the rule for survival.

* * * * *

Carbon Monoxide Poisioning

5 Men were found dead in a closed garage from carbon Monoxide poisoning. All had significant levels of the drug known as ECSTASY in their system. The drug ecstasy produces a severe of euphoria on safety while impairing judgment.

Bon County (St. Louis Mussorie, USA)

Transit driver DENNIS HUNDSDORFER was driving the bus down a Greenville street, when for an unknown reason there was fire from under the bus. The driver attributed his calm and decisive action to a training video he saw on how to evacuate persons in a burning bus. As a result 5 elderly people and an eight year old on the bus escaped without harm. The bus was a charred hulk after the fire on Wednesday June 20, 2001. Driver said I was a calm as a cucumber until I got here in the center later and started thinking about what could have happened.

* * * * *

There had been an accident in which an automobile at a slow speed of 10 MPH hit a boy. The boy fell down on his back and blood was flowing down his nostrils.

The policeman, who came immediately, insisted in not moving the body. The boy died with few minutes. Autopsy was performed and the reason for death was found to be aphiscation of lung due to blood flowing into the lungs and not the impact of accident. The policemen felt guilty, as he could have saved the boy by just turning him over and cleared his throat even though it is against standard rules. So using common sense is very essential.

* * * * *

Date: 28th march, 2006 Tuesday

The car in which Dr. Nithyanandan was traveling was involved in an accident near Velachery (Chennai). He was taken to a nearby hospital. They could not treat him, because necessary facilities were not available. Then he was taken to General Hospital. It was too late and he died on the way to hospital.

Even though help was available, it did not match to the requirement. Developing data bank of all hospitals with details of facilities available and furnishing them to all ambulances would help in saving many lives.

* * * * *

One September afternoon in 1968, a tanker carrying a load of 23000 liters of acetone, a highly dangerous liquid even trickier than petrol was unloading the cargo in a filling station.

The vehicle caught fire while emptying the last tank. The driver immediately disconnected the supply line and moved the vehicle. He drove for about 20 kilometers in 30 minutes determined to save hundreds of human lives that were threatened. He drove the potential bomb through a peaceful countryside. If took 20 minutes of hosing and pumping thousands of liters of water to cool the red-hot tank. By his presence of mind and brave action he saved a lot of human lives and properties.

* * * * *

Make the city road safe for motorists.

- Instant data about availability of blood group and blood bank matching.

- Matching of available facilities in hospitals with injuries in Road Accidents.

- Summoning of nearest Ambulance Traffic Trauma Centers with facilities and accident spots.

All such information can be given in the form of a map or list to the Ambulances and traffic police booths and trauma centers and notified public places.

* * * * *

Place: G. N. Chetty Road, T. Nagar, Chennai-600017.

Date and time: 29th October 2006 night (Chennai had one of heaviest rain fall on that day and night)

Three persons Balakrishnan (age 38), Arumugam (age 21), Balachandran (age28) were inside a Hyundai santro car. They were trapped in the rain and remained inside the car with door glasses raised to avoid getting wet. Balakrishnan informed his relative Deepu about this in the night. Next morning when Deepu went to find out about the car, he found them lying inside the car probably unconscious. On opening of the vehicle they were found in dead condition. Post mortem was carried out in Royapettah hospital, and later detailed study of the heart ventricles, it was found out, that they died due to carbon monoxide poisoning. When carbon monoxide is absorbed by the red carpasules in the blood they become toxic and cannot absorb oxygen. Death occurs within 3 minutes. The poisoning is instantaneous.

A professor of automobile engineering in IIT Chennai and his team investigated the reason for death.

They placed leak detectors inside the car and started the engine and air conditioning system and ran the vehicle for 20 hours. With all doors closed and windows raised, no carbon monoxide entered the passenger compartment.

Then they placed some lighted incense sticks in front of the A.C blower fan and the vehicle was started and ac switched on the perfume was entering the passenger compartment through ac blower fan.

It was concluded that exhaust gases from some other vehicle standing in front of the car must have entered through the ac blower fan as the ac was switched on, and caused the asphyxiation.

The passengers could have saved themselves, just by opening the doors or lowering the door glasses. Probably they were affected by carbon monoxide poisoning too soon and did not realize the effect. For them getting wet would have been a better option, as it would have saved their lives.

* * * * *

CASE: staff driving company car may not get accident claim.

This is as per the Supreme Court ruling. Mr. Chandra variyal Regional manager of a company while driving/traveling in the company car died in an accident.

The family lodged a claim under sec 166 of motor vehicle act stating company driver Mahmood Hasan was driving the car in a rash and negligent manner, which resulted in the accident and death.

Lower court gave orders for compensation to the family to the insurance company (M/s Oriental Insurance Company.)

The insurance company appealed in the Supreme Court, Supreme Court observed that the claimants (family of chandra variyal) could not prove that the driver Mahmood Hasan was driving the car at the time of accident And hence the claim made by the family of the deceased is not admissible.

Only if claim is made under sec 163 A of MV act, a person is not required to establish charge of negligence.

It is an important judgment, which proves the case has not been prepared correctly, even though it is a very deserving case for compensation.

A word of caution when you are driving a company provided car make sure you are adequately covered under the insurance policy which will safe guard you and your family.

Man steals 26 cars to meet his girl friend.

Los Angeles: whenever Antonio Moreno wanted to see his girl friend, the police say, he will jump in a car and drive right over.

But there was a problem, the 26 cars Antonio jumped into all belonged to some one else. He was behind the wheel of a 1987 TOYOTA CAMRY, when police arrested him.

He did not have a driving license or a car of his own.

* * * * *

Costly Numbers

A non-resident INDIAN from U.K Mr. Santok singh paid Rs. 4,80,000/- to get Special number CH-04-0001 for his C class MERCEDES BENZ.

Highest amount paid for a number is Rs. 5,05,000/- for the number CH-03-0001.

In CHANDIGARH (union territory). The average cost of getting a special number is almost equal to the cost of a mid sized car.

The above is nothing when compared to the recent auction of special number conducted at Emirates palace hotel, Abu Dhabi on 16th February 2008. NUMBER 1 fetched a whooping 52 crore rupees. SAEED AL KHOURI, a businessman in ABU DHABI won the auction. A total of 96 crores was collected in the auction for numbers. The amount is to be used for constructing a super specialty hospital for accident victims in Abu Dhabi. Incidentally this beats the previous record of highest amount paid by Talal ali Mohammad Khouri (Cousin of Saeed Al Khouri), who paid 25.2 Crores for a number 5 plate.

Cost of the number plate is many times higher than the cost of the car.

Aroud the World on a Scooter

73 years old MAJOR GEN. R.K. JAIN travels on his 100cc scooter often.

He traveled 9000 Km from INDIA to ENGLAND in 33 days 8000 Km from INDIA to AUSTRALIA in 38 days 4000 Km from DELHI to CHENNAI.

He covers 300 Km every day and does yoga and exercise to keep away from back ache. Always wears helmet with chinstrap.

He demonstrates age is not the criterion for travel and that too safely.

* * * * *

Mr. Thomas is an employee of accountant general office Kerala, where he was serving as assistant accounts officer. He was driving his scooter in Trivandrum near bakery junction. There was a manhole, which was opened up for some repairs, but not closed after repairs. Thomas's scooter dashed against the lid of the manhole and he was seriously injured. He was admitted in the hospital where he succumbed to the injuries because of the accident.

The repair works were assigned to a private contractor. After repairs were completed, the contractor's employees did not close the manhole. This was proved during the enquiry. In addition he has not kept any cautionary board for warning the road users, and there were no road lights burning in that stretch. The Kerala high court that tried the case has ordered a compensation of 25,00,000 Rupees with interest at the rate of 6% per annum and awarded total compensation of 32,00,000 Rupees.

Awarding the compensation is very much in favor of the deceased's family. But the family can be financially secure only when the compensation is paid to them. Like in most of the cases, when the bereaved family will receive the compensation, is a serious issue. Unless the amount is paid in time it looses it's utility.

* * * * *

The sixteen-day ordeal of John Vihtelic.

Date: September 111976, 6 o'clock in the evening.

John Vihtelic was traveling in a station wagon in an unknown route in Gilford Pinochat national park (USA). After two hours of driving in treacherous mountain road, he dozed of for a fraction of a second. A split second later, he hit a bump and plunged into darkness. Suddenly his world came apart as he lay pinned in a car wreck deep in a mountainous ravine, invisible from the road above.

His first challenge was

* To survive on what he could reach with his hands

* His second to free himself from the living grave

* He practically survived on water from a nearby spring

* He managed to free himself only on the 16 th day

* He lost more than 11 kilos of weight

* His foot was to be amputated just above his ankle

This is a typical example of traveling in an unknown route, in twilight time, and also losing concentration for a brief moment.

Every moment of driving is very important. Even a split second lapse can cost you dearly, as it happened to John.

* * * * *

Two crashes in 3 minutes.

A 43-year-Old man under influence of drinks caused two accidents in 3 minutes before getting apprehended by police. This happened in Wisconsin (USA) on 18 February 2008.

First: he ran red light while turning in a highway and hit a pick up truck.

3 Minutes later on entering another highway he hit a sport utility vehicle. This time police stopped him, before he could do more damage.

He could face criminal charges for driving under intoxicated condition and hit and run.

* * * * *

Another real life incident is narrated below

Date and time: March 23, 2008 4.30 pm (Saturday)

Mr. Prasanna Pratap, a marketing executive was traveling in a two wheeler near thirujmullaivoiyil (near avadi chennai). He was killed in a road accident. The real problem starts now. His brother who reached the spot around 5.30 pm had to run from pillar to post to get the dead body to the mortuary and get post mortem done.

Police rules say that FIR (first information report) is not sufficient for conducting post mortem... The road traffic investigation office must prepare an inquest. for which 7 witnesses are required. Prassanna's brother had to seek the help of some senior police officers help for conducting the post mortem and he could take the body of the victim on Sunday afternoon.

This is only the beginning of ordeal for prasannas family. Imagine the family lodging the accident claims and other compensation claims and getting the money.

Any accident brings agonizing periods of misery and financial and emotional strain. Without going into the details of the cause of accident, we can clearly visualize the avoidable, agonizing moments for all concerned.

* * * * *

Unusual Role of Slippers

April 07, 2008, Irumbuliur bridge on GST road.

An auto rickshaw driver Somu was traveling in a scooter with his friend who was driving the scooter. The scooter hit the median and both of them were thrown out His friend died on the spot and Somu was thrown out of the road to a nearby bush. Other road users alerted police and police arrived with an ambulance after some time. They removed the body of Sivasubramanian (Somu's friend) and were about to go. That time one of the police person noticed a pair of slippers on the roadside. They started to look for the other person. They heard moaning sound from nearby bush. After search they located Somu and he was taken to the hospital in time and he survived.

The above incident reveals an unusual role of slippers, which really saved the life of the wearer.

In life saving incidents, which are many, the timely help and assistance given by police can never be under estimated. Similarly the auto rickshaw drivers had saved many lives. In fact their contribution in life saving is very significant. Our society owes lot to their services we should see the positive side of their contribution to the society.

* * * * *

July, 2, 2001

27 year old Ramachandran living with his wife and two children in villivakkam (chennai) was hit by a stolen motor bike in which three persons were riding. He succumbed to injuries after 6 days in hospital... The claim was lodged with motor vehicles

accident tribunal. The insurance company was not willing to pay any compensation, as the vehicle involved was a stolen vehicle. Because of the efforts of a Good Samaritan lawyer MR. V.S. SURESH they could win the case.

The insurer M/S new India Assurance Company deposited a sum of RS 7 lakhs as per the tribunal order. Only in 2007 end the family was able to draw 50% of the compensation amount.

The family of Ramachandran should be thankful to the services of the good lawyer; otherwise even this compensation would not have been paid to them. The general tendency of insurer is to delay the case as much as possible and avoid paying any compensation. GOD forbid if vehicle involved was a government vehicle, the family would not have got any thing at all.

* * * * *

One more real life incident in which for no fault of theirs a family was forced into a fatal vacation.

Scene 1

TUESDAY 17, June 2008 Mr. Ravinder kulkarni of Tata precision services of Singapore, his wife shallaja, and Sons Asish and Aniket had an occasion to celebrate. The reason was, their younger son Aniket who had heart problem and was being treated at frontier lifeline hospital was examined in the hospital and declared to be fit and fine and no cause to worry. They were staying in Residency hotel in Chennai.

Scene 2

Tuesday evening 17, June 2008: They left in a call taxi for spending a well deserved holiday in Mahabalipuram, a tourist resort about 60 kilometers from Chennai. Fate decided otherwise. When they reached tiger caves, it came in the form of a drunken driver, Sivaguru. He rammed his vehicle into the car in which Kulkarni family was traveling. Ravinder kulkarni, his son Aniket and driver of the car died instantly. His wife Shallaja succumbed to the injuries later. Only his elder son Asish survived, and his agony will continue for the rest of his life having seen his dear ones dying in front of him.

Killer driver sivaguru sustained minor injuries and being treated in a city hospital. Can he undo the damages and agony he had caused to the family?

The fact remains that driver sivaguru was not an enemy to kulkarnies, but inadvertently became the cause of their misfortune, the real culprit is the drinks, which made sivaguru to convert the luxury of a car into a mad bull elephant. We have no right to drink and drive and cause misery to any body. Because of the negligence of one drunken driver one whole familie's life was ruined. Here we cannot forget the driver of kulkarni's car. He also became a victim.

As we cannot reconstruct the accident scene, we cannot say whether the accident could have been avoided... But the point remains whether the driver of Kulkarni's vehicle made allowance for the stupidity of the drunken driver. This is a million rupee question?

Figuratively Speaking

1. Economic loss due to road accidents in India every year 55000 Crores

2. Longest highway in the world – PAN American Highway 24140 Km

3. Highest motor able Road KHARDUNGLAPASS, LADAKH, KHARDUNGLA1'ASS, LADAKH, J&K. INDIA – 18640 feet Above sea level

4. Largest bus fleet Andra Pradesh Road Transport Corporation 18397 buses

5. Lowest RoadIsrael Road Israel – shores of dead sea 1289 feet below sea level

6. No. of Vehicles per 1000 persons in USA 850

7. Loss of fuel lost in evaporation in USA every year 150 million liters

8. No. of fatal accidents in a year 100 thousand

9. No. of passengers Traveling in Bus everyday in Chennai 46 lacs

10. Total length of roads in India 33 lacs Kms

11. No. of persons using two wheelers. Auto Rickshaw 29 lacs

12. Fuel consumption in US per day 20 million barrels

13. No. of vehicles in Chennai 18 lacs

14. No. of vehicles per 1000 persons in India 17

15. One vehicle is stolen in India per every 15 minutes

16. No. of persons getting injured every year in India 10 lacs

17. No. of vehicles in India 5 crores

18. Most precious thing in the world for you 1 (your own life)

Consequences of Accidents

One of the best ways to ensure your continued health is to avoid automobiles. Each time you drive or walk along the street, you trust your life to strangers driving all forms of automobiles. Automobile related accidents injure and kill more frequently than lightning.

Again a small anecdote.

One person driving a motorcycle hits another in the street. The pedestrian is injured. Two wheelers rider says 'Oh God' I would like to take you to the nearest doctor.

The pedestrian: says 'I am the doctor.' Then pedestrian says I would like to consult a nearby lawyer for compensation. The two wheelers rider says 'I am the lawyer.' The above incident may not be uncommon. Jokes apart, it explains both medical and legal angles of an accident.

Most surprising commonality among all is no body wants an accident. In Telco, as soon as you enter the factory premises, you find a big board 'we welcome everybody except Mr. & Mrs. Accident!'

Accidents do not happen they are caused.

Accidents come without any pre-warning.

Accidents are caused within fraction of a second, much before those who are involved realize it.

Now the crux of the problem. No body wants it, still it had occurred much against everybody's wishes.

In Any Accident

- You may be the cause of an accident either knowingly or Unknowingly.

- It may be fatal or non fatal.

- One or many people including pedestrian may be injured seriously or sustained minor injures.

- One or more vehicles be involved in the primary as secondary collision. The secondary collision is the result of the initial or first collision.

- Properties belonging to the govt. or private parties may be damaged.

- You may be the victim of an accident for no fault of yours. Whatever be the reason, it affects you and your vehicle.

Ensure

- Vehicle is comprehensively insured and valid at the time of accident. All papers of the vehicle are in order.

- You or the person who is driving the vehicle is in possession of a valid driving license for the vehicle being driven.

- The driver is not under influence of alcohol or any other form of drug.

- You have not done anything, which is prohibited by law that may disqualify you from any compensation.

In the event of any accident of any nature, your interests are safe guarded by insurance company to a very great extent. Never underestimate the value of having valid and adequate insurance cover.

As per the judgment of the supreme court given recently it is the responsibility of the owner to ensure before appointing a driver either part or full time, that he/she is in possession of a valid driving license to drive the type of vehicle they are authorized to drive. Failure of ensuring this will absolve the insurance companies of any liability that may arise out of any accident in which your vehicle may be involved either directly or indirectly. The owner of the vehicle will be solely responsible to pay any compensation to the aggrieved party/or parties.

Having proper insurance and complying with all provisions will indemnify you from practically everything.

What are the actions to be taken in the event of any unfortunate accidents are given in the chapter of insurance. However some important points are given now.

1. Most Important: Never admit any liability either verbally or in writing. Let the insurance company do everything. They are equipped and meant for it.

2. Inform all events to the insurance company and keep a record of all communication for future. Never give wrong, incomplete, incorrect information.

3. Lodge first information report in nearest police station. This will save you of many future problems.

4. Consult a lawyer who is your well wisher. A good and reliable lawyer can be of great help and can help you

in getting medical treatment repairing your car and negotiate with insurancea company, police in sorting out post accident problems.

5. Whatever be your role in any accident, remember you are entitled to get proper compensation. The compensation should neither be pittance (too little) nor a bonanza (too much).

Some important and relevant time frames for various contingences pertaining to automobile accidents are given in the following paragraphs.

Always remember if you are a victim of an automobile accident, you are entitled for compensation, medical treatment and any other damages to your properties.

The Supreme Court had delivered many landmark judgments on accident related cases.

First is earlier time limit for filing cases within 6 months is relaxed. In case of hit and run cases, the police and transport authorities must find the culprit and book then under relevant penal codes.

Stringent checks on plying of non insured vehicles.

Not having valid or possession of forged license will not be reason for rejection of claim as long as there is no foul play on the part of the owner.

Govt. agencies can be booked and penalized for willful negligence in maintaining roads, which becomes accident-Prone.

Severe punishment for drunken driving. In another case the CEO of a reputed company was booked for rash and negligent driving causing death of many pavement dwellers.

The following organizations are dealing with motor related accidents.

1. Insurance ombudsman for viewing insurance claims in case of disputes.

2. Consumer courts having jurisdiction or states and union territories.

3. Motor vehicles accident Tribunal.

4. High courts and Supreme Court.

5. immediate redressal for aggrieved persons by way of interim compensation. pending final orders.

6. Free legal aid service for victims without financial position to fight the case.

7. Various hospitals and 24-hour trauma centers are notified, in each city and states. They will render all assistance in case of road accidents.

8. Traffic and police maintaining law and order will render all help in case of accidents by way of evacuation to nearby hospitals and ensure all connected vehicles are properly identified and necessary markings are made on accident sites, which will form record for future.

9. Many NGO's like Lions; Rotary clubs are operating free blood banks to help accident victims. They have placed ambulances at important accident-prone locations.

10. All details are regularly published in local newspapers and magazines.

11. Automobile Association of India are having offices all over India. They will help all motorists who are members and also all involved in local accidents whenever possible.

12. Various 24 × 7, help lines are available in websites, which can be accessed in any Internet facilities.

13. Free telephones for informing accident cases such as 108 are available. Any public persons can notify police. They need not reveal their name. They will not be asked to testify at later stage.

We know very well that you are not given a second chance, to replay an accident scene. Presently lot of scientific research is going on to establish the true reasons of accident. Various vehicle accident reconstruction methods are being used.

The purpose is to estimate in both qualitative and quantitative manner, how an accident had occurred. Reconstructions are done based on the evidence gathered during investigation. Whether accident is between two or more vehicles or vehicle and pedestrians or vehicle and a barrier. The study is divided into pre impact; impact and post impact components and studied in thorough detail. Three main factors human, vehicle and environment are taken into account during investigation. The purpose is to establish all possible reasons and circumstances, which led to the accident.

This is done not for the purpose of apportioning the blame on some agency. The findings will be of great value in design of vehicles and establishing the pattern of human behavior. They will of immense value for future generation road users. They can learn from the faults of others and improve their ability to cope up with many uncertain situations.

It is the bounden duty and obligation for everybody to render all help and assistance in case of any unfortunate accident whether minor or major. Someday we may badly be in need of such help.

Important Milestones

In transport Sector in INDIA

1897 – India had its first automobile (car)

1898 – India had four cars, one with JAMSHED JI TATA – INDUSTRIALIST, second with RUSTOM CAMA_SOLICITOR, third with COWASJI WADIA_MERCHANT, fourth with PACK_ JWELLER

1903 – First vehicle produced in INDIA by M/s SIMPSON & CO

1905 – First lot of 304 cars were registered in MUMBAI

1908 – French motor, KOLKATTA, had started, first driving school of motoring

1909 – First taxis in MUMBAI and KALKOTTA

1912 – Famous TVS company was-started

1914 – First motor vehicle act

1920 - INDIA had 13486 cars

1927 – The INDIAN roads committee under chairmanship of Mr. Jayakar

1928 – First indigenously assembled car in INDIA – by General motors

1948 – Hindustan motors, Asoke Leyland, Standard motors started

1950 – motor vehicle taxation highest in the world

1953 – First vanguard assembled in standard motors CHENNAI

1983 – Liberalization in policies regarding manufacturing of automobiles ancillaries was announced by government of INDIA. In fact 1983 was the watershed for all transport related sector development

After 1983, the development of automobile and transport industry had been phenomenal.

2006 to 2016 – Government of INDIA had launched ambitious AUTOMOTIVE VISION PLAN.

2008 Very important milestone in automobile industry. Mr. RATAN TATA, chairman of TATA group industries unveiled.

INDIA"S proudest car NOVA. The famous rupee ONE LAKH car. He proved to the world that INDIA can produce such cars with their own technology. This was unveiled in AUTO EXPO 2008 in NEW DELHI on 10th January 2008. With this remarkable achievement he can be called as HENRY FORD OF INDIA.

2008 JUNE 18 FIRST hybrid petrol electric car HONDA CIVIC. Introduced in INDIA.

Addresses of Important Organizations

Most Important Information. Indian Govt Had declared number 108. As Universal No for al emergencies through out India. This is a Toll free number. This will be great help in all forms of Emergencies.

It is not possible to list out all organizations dealing with road safety at that itself will become separate book.

Over the years lots of developments had taken place in Govt. Policies, Road construction, Vehicle Development and other allied fields.

Since it is a continuous process, my request to all readers is to keep them well informed about them. They will be of great help in time of need.

No of voluntary agencies, hospitals and medical professional skills and Traffic Management methods, have come into play in Reduction of ill effects of Road usage.

But population explosion and exponential increase of vehicles had off set the benefits considerably.

Best recipe for ensuring your own safety and that of others are

- ➤ Keep yourself updated of latest rules and other relevant details of all places. They will be handy while tavelling.

- ➤ Train your children, friends, Relatives about safety in Road usage.

> ➤ Render all possible help to the needy when they are in dire need.

> ➤ Set an example of proper and safe usage. Road user in any form are subjected to risks. Use sound common sense at all times.

The Top Ten James Bond Cars

1. Roger Moore – CITREON ZCV – For your eyes only – 1981

2. Sean Connery – Austin Martin-Gold finger – 1964

3. Pierce Bronson – T-55 battle tank St peters berg-Golden eye – 1995

4. Roger Moore – AMC Hornet-x-hatch back-in Thailand – man with a golden gun 1974

5. Roger Moore – Lotus sprit – the spy who loved me – 1997

6. Timothy Dalton – drug filled tanker-License to kill – 1989

7. Pierce Bronson – Remote controlled BMW 750 – tomorrow Never dies-1997

8. Sean Connery – Sun Beam – DR – 1962

9. Timothy Dalton – Aston martin-v-8S vantage-Living Day light – 1984

10. Pierce Bronson – Aston Martin-vanquish-v-12 – die another Day – 2002

Cars speak

1. Maruti   –   Count on us

2. Hyundai   –   Drive your way

3.	Ford	–	Make every day exciting
4.	Honda	–	Out perform
5.	GM Chevrolet	–	for special journey called life
6.	Skoda	–	Obsessed with quality since 1885
7.	Toyota	–	All you desire moving forward
8.	Nissan	–	Stay update
9.	BMW	–	Ultimate driving machine
10.	Benz	–	Legendary unlike any other
11.	Volkswagen	–	Driver wanted
12.	Subaru	–	Think, feel, drive
13.	KIA	–	Power to surprise
14.	Mercury	–	New door opened
15.	Audi	–	Never follow
16.	Mitsubishi	–	wake up drive
17.	Bajaj	–	Inspiring confidence
18.	Suzuki (motor cycle)	–	Mark your presence

Bumper Stickers

Very funny, Scotty, now beam down my clothes

If you are physic – think, honk

If you can read this, I can slam my brakes and sue you

Forget world peace, visualize your turn signal

Do not drink and drive – you may hit a bump and spill it

Honk as much as you can – I am loading my gun

I am not tense – just terribly, terribly alert

Ten Commandments from Vatican for Motorists

Vatican had issued Ten Commandments for motorists. This once again proves that the slogan 'drive safe and be safe' is for all people of the world and crosses all barriers of nation, gender, age, religion etc.

- Thou shall not kill

- The road shall be for you as a means of communion between people and not of mortal harm

- Courtesy, uprightness and prudence will help you deal with unforeseen events

- Be charitable and help your neighbor in need, especially victims of accidents

- Cars shall not be for you an expression of power and domination and an occasion of sin

- Charitably convince the young and not so young not to drive when they are not in a fitting condition to do so

- Support families of accident victims

- Bring guilty motorists and their victims together, at the appropriate time, so that they can undergo the liberating experience of forgiveness

- On the road, protect the more vulnerable party

- Feel responsible toward others

Executive Summary

This chapter summarizes essence of this book for quick reference and action. This should be read and reread till they become part of us.

A. Always consider safety in your thought and action. Be alert. Never abuse your privilege as road user in any form.

B. Brakes: they are vital. Keep the system in fully reliable state. You do not know when you will need them.

C. Children: you owe your life to them. Never make them victims of your mistakes.

D. DRIVE SAFE BE SAFE: let the theme of this book be your primary consideration as road user.

E. Exhaust: Remember; what comes out of the tail pipe is important. Take care of your vehicle. You have no right to make other people suffer due to your faults.

F. Fasteners (bolts and nuts) Remember however big you (your vehicle) are a small fastener can make the difference between life and death.

G. Guard yourself: against other's mistakes it is the best way to protect yourself.

H. Horn: never demand your right by misuse. It is not meant to scare others. Use judiciously.

I. Instruments: every instrument has a story to tell. Be thorough with knowledge of all indications.

J. Jaywalker: beware of careless walker on the road. They are irresponsible and accident-prone.

K. Key: keep duplicate key in a safe but accessible place for emergency use. In case original is lost make duplicate key immediately.

L. Lights: in automobiles lights are the only means of communication between drivers and other road users. Most of the highway accidents are either due to too much glaring lights or very poor lighting. Keep all lights in good working condition as every light has a specific function. Headlights should be properly focused.

M. Maintenance: most important to ensure safe, reliable and trouble free performance.

N. Never succumb to temptations in violating any traffic safety rules. They are your lifesavers.

O. Oxygen: engine also requires oxygen as you do. Keep air filters Clean, so that they do not suffocate.

P. Pollution is slow poison for every one. Contribute your might to reduce and eliminate the menace.

Q. Queue: Never jump the queue in traffic junctions and endanger yourself – and others.

R. Remember there is no reconstruction of any accident. You do not have proverbial cat's life.

S. Speed: Limit your speed. Remember there is no safe speed. Full speed is fool's speed.

T. Traffic sense. Develop strong logical traffic sense. Anticipate other's move and safe guard yourself.

U. Unacquainted terrains: never travel in unacquainted routes, particularly in night. (Get all possible information before venturing).

V. Vibration: be observant on any vibration in vehicle due to loose or broken parts. Remember vibration feeds on vibration and ultimate brakeage.

W. Wear seat belts. Wear helmets while driving and traveling in two wheelers. It is life saving.

X. Xmas: plan holiday travels in advance. Make provision for heavy, unruly traffic and drunken drivers for your own safety.

Y. You are the most important person in your life. As proper road user you can set an example to others.

Z. Zebra crossings are best crossings. Always use them for your own safety. Motorists – respect zebra crossings. Pedestrians – use only zebra crossings.

Never misuse. Show consideration to elderly, handicapped persons.

Executive Summary

♦ **This chapter summarizes essence of this book for quick reference and action. They should be read and reread till they become part of us.**

♦ You may be the road user in any form. Be safe; never take chance. You are the only one who can ensure this for your self.

♦ Driving a motor vehicle is a privilege and not a right. It takes skill, common sense and thorough knowledge of rules and regulations found in the law.

♦ Because of age, senior citizens become both cause and consequence of accidents. They deserve considerations in all respects.

♦ Not sleeping for 24 hours prior to driving is akin to drunken driving.

♦ Remember alcoholic effects reach the brain within five minutes after drinking.

♦ Majority of two wheelers in India are owned and driven by teenagers and persons below 30 years of age. Teenagers are most accident phone.

♦ Most of the devices of the vehicles will not hurt you, unless you go out of the way to hurt yourself.

- Proper and timely maintenance will ensure vehicle reliability, safety in use, reduced running and maintenance costs. Above all it will give us the satisfaction of possessing an asset we can be proud of.

- Best recipe for trouble and accident free vehicle is a well maintained vehicle and safe and mature driver.

- Remember your own life and that of others is more important than the difference in cost, between original genuine parts and spurious parts.

- On an average man in cities inhale noxious gases equivalent to smoking 10 packets of cigarettes a day. In case you are smoker or user of tobacco in any form add this to your daily consumption. Ensure your contribution to reduce pollution.

- Save your own life and those who travel with you the driver's role starts only when he or she starts driving, after they get their driving license. Every moment of driving is important.

- The most expensive fragrance in the world is new car smell. Consumers are willing to spend lakhs of rupees for that smell.

- Every 3 minutes a car is stolen. 40000 cars are being stolen every year in India. If auto theft were legitimate business it will rank 50th among fortune 500 companies.

- INDIA can boast of highest motor able road in the world at highest point it climbs 5682 meters (18640 feet). This is held in GUINNESS BOOK OF WORLD RECORDS.

- Unhappy feature in a cycle is a large number of accidents are associated with it. It is because it offers no protection to the rider in the event of any accident or collision.

- Always carry identification papers and important medical information about you. Suffering from diabetes, allergy to any particular drugs etc. they will be your lifesaver in case of any unfortunate accident.

- Future cars (Rs. 1 lac car) are likely to bridge the gap between two wheelers and mid sized car. Even with small family norms requirement of cars are increasing day by day.

- Because of constant changing external factors, maintaining climate control in the automobile requires extremely efficient system.

- Accident is defined as absence of purpose in the succession of events. Nothing is likely to test one's knowledge of first aid more than accidents suffered on highways.

- Nearly any one of sound mind and body can learn to drive a car/vehicle. But to drive safely and well with consideration, it is an art and only begins after the driving test is over.

- In the event of any accident of any nature, your interests are safe guarded by insurance companies to a very great extent. NEVER under estimate the value of having valid and adequate insurance cover. It will indemnify you from practically every thing. Never admit any liability, in the event of any accident. Let the insurance company do it for you. Select known company for insurance and clear all doubts as soon as you receive the policy. Have a reliable lawyer as your friend.

♦ It is the bounden duty and obligation for everybody to render all help in case of any unfortunate accident, whether minor or major. Some day we may badly in need of such help.

♦ Learn first aid particularly Cardio pulmonary resuscitation from any of the training agencies like hospitals. You will become one of the most useful person in case of any emergency.

♦ Remember there is nothing known as minor detail in the automobile. Every part is important and even smallest part can cause major accident.

Illustrations

In the following pages, a few illustrations are given. They give you an insight of various issues in a pictorial form. Some of them are funny, but no Doubt they help you to realize the inherent dangers. We can learn many useful Lessons. Pictures convey better meaning than words.

Spot at least one difference

LENS VIEW

On the pedals of peril...Pic. by T.A.Hafeez.

Circus on road

Dear Reader

WE may not meet in person. In this book we met. So I take this opportunity to convey my best wishes for a happy, Sane and Safe Road use.

LET THE ALMIGHTY be with you, and guide you always. Every moment of driving or using the road in any form is important. It can make tremendous difference in your life and lives of your family Members.

Let safety be your watchword always.

Good luck to all readers.

We Believe

SUN is 148 million kilometers away and sunlight takes 8 minutes, 20 seconds to reach earth.

Average distance of MOON is 372144 kilometers from earth. Diameter of earth is 12672 kilometers, and so on.

But when a park bench is painted and the sign says "wet paint do not touch," we make sure of it and get paint stuck on our fingers.

We mistrust the obvious, like wise as road users, we tend to' ignore the obvious safety precautions.

Every road accident if truthfully investigated will prove the above point beyond any doubt.

There is no truly unavoidable accident. Accidents are formed in less than 3 seconds, much before those involved realize it. There is no reconstruction or retake in any accident.

With this book in your hands, you are becoming part of the solution, to the Perplexing problem. By ensuring your safety, you are ensuring others safety as well.

Accidents do not discriminate victims.

If you want to realize the true effect of any accident, just close your eyes, and imagine yourself or your dear ones involved in a motor related Accident, vividly feel the effects it has on YOU.

DO IT NOW AND FEEL THE EFFECT. You will automatically become a safe and sane road user. And a good will ambassador on road.

AND THAT EXACTLY, 1S THE PURPOSE OF THIS BOOK.

www.ingramcontent.com/pod-product-compliance
Lightning Source LLC
Chambersburg PA
CBHW021349210526
45463CB00001B/42